PLATE I

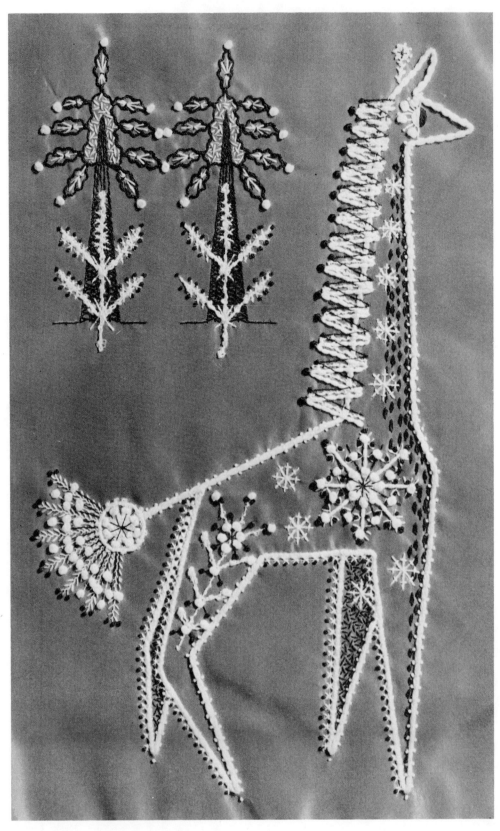

'Giraffe' showing different weights of threads and weaving yarns

CREATIVE STITCHES

Edith John

DOVER PUBLICATIONS, INC.
NEW YORK

TO MY STUDENTS

Acknowledgment

In compiling this book of stitches, I acknowledge with gratitude and thanks the encouragement I have received from my parents and students, and the enthusiastic help of Mr Eric Platt, ARCA, and Mrs Platt. My thanks are offered to all those who have so readily allowed me to use photographs of their embroidery, and who eagerly tried new ideas of mine and suggested variations of their own. I am also indebted to Mr Desmond Byrne and Mr Alec Hainsworth for the excellent photographs with which this book is illustrated.

E. J.

Published in Canada by General Publishing Company, Ltd., 30 Lesmill Road, Don Mills, Toronto, Ontario.
Published in the United Kingdom by Constable and Company, Ltd., 10 Orange Street, London WC 2.

This Dover edition, first published in 1973, is an unabridged republication of the work first published in 1967. This edition is published through special arrangement with B. T. Batsford, Ltd., 4 Fitzhardinge Street, London, the original publishers.

International Standard Book Number: 0-486-22972-6
Library of Congress Catalog Card Number: 73-84802

Manufactured in the United States of America
Dover Publications, Inc.
180 Varick Street
New York, N.Y. 10014

Contents

PLATE II
'Scarecrow' by Joan Cooke, worked with Wheatear
stitch only

PLATE III

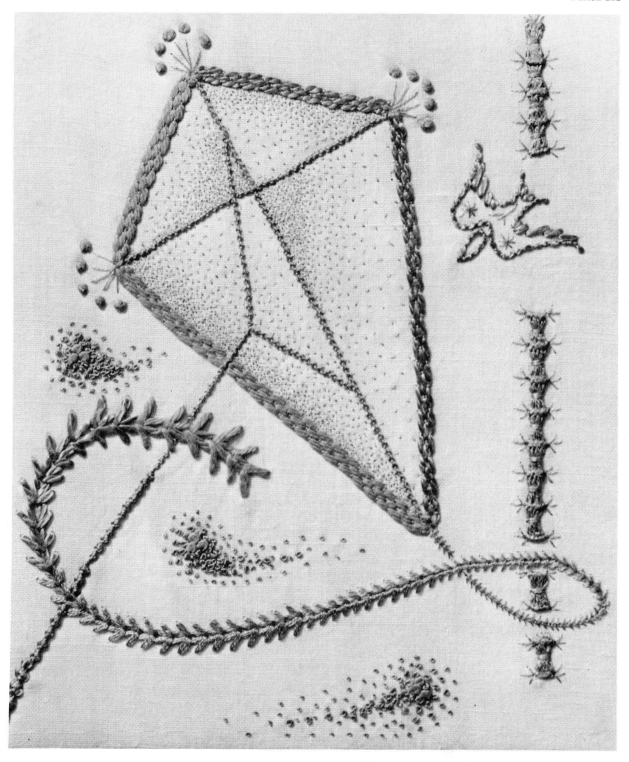

'Kite' by Joan Cooke, worked with different weights of thread in one colour only

PLATE IV

'The King' by Doris Warr.
A string doodle or trial run
for extended couching

'The King' by Doris Warr. Gold extended couching

Introduction

In spite of the wealth of stitches and methods which present-day embroiderers have inherited from the past, the need is often felt for a new way in which to interpret modern designs. Surely this is a good thing, because if embroidery is to be a living art, it must speak in the idiom of the twentieth century. There are many who believe that in order to create something which is new in needlework it is necessary to sacrifice both skill and taste. That this is not so is clearly evident when one studies the beautiful pieces of work which are being produced in abundance today.

A study of historical examples will convince most people that in every age, and indeed in every country, stitches, methods and styles of design have changed with the changing times, and that contemporary embroiderers are simply following a great and glorious tradition.

Stitches, to the embroiderer, are a never-failing source of delight. They are the means by which fabrics and threads are brought together in perfect harmony, and by which the simplest design is given life. In the hands of a skilful person even the cheapest materials and the coarsest threads have their value increased beyond measure, and the most beautiful ones are made to resemble that garment of light which is sometimes glimpsed with the inward eye, but which is always, tantalizingly, just beyond one's reach.

It is for the benefit of the countless embroiderers who love stitchery that this book has been written.

Experimental Embroidery

To embroider means to enrich with needlework, and embroidery is the art of producing such ornamentation. Without a knowledge of stitches no needlework is possible, as stitches of some kind are necessary for the production of even the simplest form of embroidery. They are the means by which the needlewoman expresses herself, and, in so doing, if she has understanding plus an inventive turn of mind, she will produce work which is both pleasing and original. Far from being a dull chore, the mastery of stitches, and particularly the discovery of their possibilities, should be an exciting adventure of the kind which appeals to the embroiderer of every degree of skill, from the beginner of any age to the professional worker whose attainments act only as a spur to further experiments.

Once the basic movements of needle and thread have been mastered, i.e. flat stitchery, looping, chaining and knotting, it is an easy step to the production of variations on these themes, and to the discovery of entirely new stitch forms. Generally speaking, the simplest stitches offer more possibilities for development than the very complicated ones, and it is a great mistake to spurn the simple ones just because they are easy to work. It must be remembered that if the beauty of stitches is to be shown to full advantage, even the humblest ones demand all the skill and care of which the embroideress is capable.

A mistake in the working of a stitch is not always a major disaster, indeed it often proves to be the starting point of an effective variation. The combination of two or more well-known stitches might result in something which is fresh and pleasing.

Planned irregularities in the length of stitches, deliberate omissions in filling and line stitches, and a sudden change of direction of an important movement will all give surprisingly interesting results.

Nor should other sources of inspiration for new stitches be neglected. For instance, the back of all embroidery should be studied carefully. Many line and filling stitches are lovely on the reverse side, and the creative needlewoman will be quick to make use of this almost unlimited source of supply. All darned fillings can be reversed easily, but the back stitch fillings are much more exciting. From this simple reversing of easy stitches, it is a short step to reversing whole pieces of work. Canvas work, especially that which is worked only in orthodox stitchery, often looks much more interesting on the under side, and so, too, do some pieces of machine embroidery. The development of machine techniques must surely encourage the hand worker to experiment still further. She will find that it is not necessary to make a slavish copy of machine work in order to produce new stitchery, in fact it would be valueless to do so. Woven and printed textiles, canework, and the patterns on many natural forms, are other sources from which ideas for new stitches can be taken, and so, of course, are the historical embroideries which are to be found in museums and private collections all over the country.

Stitches should not be placed in firmly labelled compartments. Many so called canvas stitches make delightful drawn fabric work when they are placed on a suitable background. Border and line stitches, whether raised or flat, make attractive fillings on any kind of material. Lace stitches can be used as edges and insertions; and drawn thread patterns worked on all kinds of fabric if a base of bars is worked first.

The question now arises, is it necessary to fill any given shape completely with stitches? Naturally, method has some bearing on the answer, and so, too, has purpose. For instance, canvas upholstery must be hard wearing as well as attractive, and it is not wise to leave large areas of the canvas uncovered. But small pieces of unadorned fabric add to the interest of the work and do not detract from its durability. At the other end of the scale, drawn fabric embroidery calls for a looser treatment, and here it is possible to work lines of irregular length and to leave portions of the shapes unworked.

These rest spaces enhance the beauty of the fillings and often help to turn a very simple design into something which is quite out of the ordinary. Couched fillings, buttonhole fillings, black work and surface stitchery are only a few of the methods which look most attractive when treated in this manner.

Many lovely pieces of embroidery lack vitality because hard and heavy outlines isolate one shape from another. Outlines should excite interest; they should ebb and flow, adding depth and character to the work, and sometimes they should be slipped to one side or dispensed with altogether, so as to allow one filling to merge into another.

Fillings, of course, are not always required, and many designs look really impressive when they are worked with line stitches only. Broad and narrow, flat and raised, smooth and knotted, with so many to choose from even lines need not be dull. To change the stitch halfway round a shape enlivens an otherwise monotonous line, and it becomes even more attractive if the stitch is changed at irregular intervals, according to the scale of the design and the thickness of the thread. A feeling of depth can be obtained by contrasting one thick outline with several fine ones. This can be done either by changing the kind of thread, or by working a few rows of one stitch close together on one part of a line, and only one row of the same stitch on other parts. Having decided that fillings are not always necessary, and that outlines may, at times, be dispensed with, we have now to decide whether it is possible to produce an interesting piece of work with only one stitch. History answers in the affirmative, and it is possible to see examples from almost every corner of the world which prove how attractive this method can be. From China we have pieces worked solely in satin stitch, and India has given us glorious embroideries worked in simple chain stitch. English tent stitch panels of the sixteenth century are quite well known, and in peasant embroideries we find pieces worked in double knot, or double chain or closed herringbone, to the exclusion of all others.

Today we often feel a little more adventurous than our ancestors, and make use of any stitch which can be 'broken down' easily. Wheatear stitch can be used as a line, a filling, a shading and a powdering, and so, too, can fly stitch. Both give delightfully modern effects, but the roots of this idea are in the past.

One of the most interesting modern methods, extended couching, excludes outlines of any sort, and helps the embroiderer to make the most of her design. She selects a point at which to begin sewing, and does not cut off her thread until the design is complete. This method calls for careful consideration, and even after doodling with a pencil on paper, a trial run with string stuck over the pencil marks might be necessary. This trial run is used mainly to give confidence to the worker, and she should not attempt to make a faithful copy of it. In order to arrive back at any given point it will be necessary for her to retrace her steps many times, and even to work over finished couching. A lovely raised effect results from all this doodling, and the work shades beautifully because the direction of the thread is changed constantly. Almost any kind of thread can be used successfully, but certain types of gold thread look simply wonderful. This kind of work needs no enrichment, and I think it is best to work the stitches in the same colour as the thread which is being couched.

Groups of stitches should not be isolated or regarded as unsuitable for anything except the purpose for which they were originally intended, and if this idea is carried to its logical conclusion, it will be realized that methods, too, can be combined quite successfully. A little careful planning and adaptation gives unexpectedly good results. For instance, cut work and appliqué combine very well, shadow work, broderie Anglaise, drawn thread and drawn ground remind us of the fine white work of the nineteenth century, and, odd as it may seem, canvas work and appliqué are extraordinarily good partners. There is so much to be done, one only needs the time, and the courage.

Although this book is concerned primarily with hand work, it must be mentioned that a combination of hand and machine embroidery is most attractive, as one is the perfect foil for the other. This is particularly true of the delicate 'free' machine embroidery, in which the sewing machine is used as a drawing tool, and the operator has complete control.

If experimental work is to result in anything worth-while, texture must be taken into account, especially when a piece of work is to be carried out in one colour only. This fascinating method calls for a high degree of skill and it must be remembered that the texture of any stitch is affected to some extent by the thread. With stranded threads it is fun to alter the tex-

ture of the work by varying the number of strands used in the needle. It is very dull to work a whole piece with the same number of strands. Even more remarkable changes in texture can be achieved by using an assortment of threads in one piece of work, always considering, of course, suitability for purpose. The choice is wide and the discriminating needlewoman will delight in using glossy silk and metal threads as a contrast to cotton and even woollen ones. She will discover the beauty of threads which are often despised, and she will have history to prove her right. With such a variety of threads from which to choose, new ways of using them will soon become apparent. Very fine threads worked over a coarse foundation thread enrich the coarse one, and sometimes refine it out of all recognition. The reverse process is occasionally successful.

Because the choice of thread makes such a difference to the appearance of the stitches, in the following chapters the effect of the thread on the new stitch forms will be discussed when the need arises.

Finally we must think about backgrounds, because without them we cannot begin to work. Although there is an ever increasing number of fabrics, which are interesting in weave and texture, glorious in colour, and of every conceivable weight, many people like to create their own backgrounds. I think it is because the background and its decoration should be as one, or because it is necessary for two articles, such as a dress and a bag, to match exactly. Hence clever craftswomen knit, crochet, print or weave fabrics for themselves. They build foundations with layers of net and other transparent fabrics, and they even destroy a fabric in order to create something new.

Holes can be singed or torn in all kinds of materials, and transparent fabrics treated in this way look lovely when mounted on a gaily coloured ground. Although it sounds a very silly idea, a glass mat was made in this way and enriched with machine embroidery and a needlepoint edge. It is firm, it looks attractive, and I am sure it will withstand a great deal of wear.

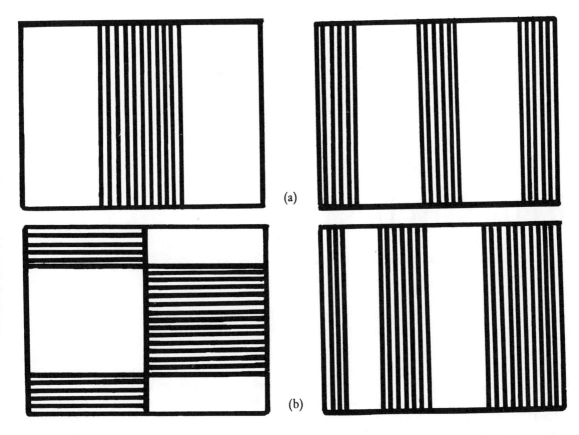

1 Paled work   (a) old   (b) new

It is possible with many fabrics to withdraw threads either singly or in groups, from warp and weft, and to darn either in threads of a different colour and texture, or strips of another kind of fabric. If a really transparent effect is required, simply withdraw more threads, and use the material as it is, or mount it on another fabric. Velvet makes a delicious under garment, as the pile rises through the spaces in the top material.

With a loosely woven fabric it is possible to pull the threads apart instead of withdrawing them. This can be done in either a formal or haphazard manner. The threads should be tied or stitched in place.

If none of the methods mentioned above is suitable, the fabric might be given a very rough texture by scribbling all over it with a sewing machine. This treatment also strengthens the ground.

Another good method is to apply pieces of fabric of the same colour, but of different textures to the ground and to link them up with either machine or by hand sewing before tracing the design. Alternatively, when the work is complete, texture parts of the background with powderings, darnings or irregular couched fillings. The sixteenth-century English method known as paled work might also be used (1). Simply join strips of fabric of different colours and textures.

These methods of preparing grounds show how essential it is for them to be regarded as part of the whole, enriching, blending, but never fighting with, or claiming supremacy over, the main theme.

Flat Stitches

Choose needles of good quality with smooth eyes, large enough to take the thread easily through the ground, but not so large as to leave a hole in the material. A needle which is too small will cause puckering, and the thread will be damaged by constant pulling.

To begin any stitch neatly is an obvious asset, and there are several ways of doing this. The first method is to make a firm knot on the thread, and to made it doubly secure with two tiny back stitches in the material at the place where the embroidery is to begin. This method is quite successful when the back of the work will never be seen, and if it is done properly it is neat and secure.

The second method, though often used, is not always neat. Make a few running stitches along the line which is to be embroidered, starting an inch or so from the beginning of the line and working up to the starting point. These stitches will be covered with embroidery, and so the end of the thread will be quite secure.

The third method is probably the neatest, and is certainly safe, but some embroiderers find it laborious. Begin to work, leaving a long end of the thread on top of the material. When sufficient stitches are in position, take the end to the back of the work and darn it neatly and firmly into the back of the embroidery.

Threads which are too coarse to pull through material in the usual manner present no problem if a hole is made with a stiletto and the end of the thread is stiffened with adhesive tape, and gently eased backwards, from the top of the work, through the hole. The tape should be removed, and the ends of the thread frayed out and oversewn to the back of the work.

To fasten off a thread, take it to the back of the work and oversew it into the stitches for a short way, ending with a tiny buttonhole stitch for extra security.

Joinings should be invisible, and if it is necessary to join a new thread to a line of stitches it must be done carefully. A few moments study of the stitch which is being worked will help the embroiderer to decide on the best point at which to end a thread (2). The new thread should be brought to the surface in exactly the same place as the old one would have done if it had not been too short (3). Never leave a thread hanging at the back of the work as it becomes entangled with the needle and often pops to the surface where it is not wanted. Leave unfinished lengths of thread on the top of the work where they can be seen. Having mastered beginnings, endings and joinings, let us begin our search for new stitch forms with stem stitch. Being a flat stitch it is easy to execute, and in its simplest forms it can be worked successfully with every kind of thread. Soft, spreading threads, either coarse or fine, give a smooth line; and round, firm threads give a ropey effect.

2

3

4 *Stem Stich* Keep the thread to the right of the needle and after picking up a small piece of material bring the needle out at the top of the preceding stitch.

5 *Alternating Stem* Change the position of the thread from left to right alternately. The needle must follow a straight course and should be brought to the surface of the material at the top of the preceding stitch.

5, 6, 7 *Alternating Stem* as a line stitch

5 the position of the thread is changed every time a new stitch is made.

6 the position is changed after making 3 plain stem stitches.

7 3 stitches, then 1, then 3 are made and the position of the thread is changed in that order.

8 and 9 It is possible to use these line stitches as border stitches, and from border stitches it is a simple matter to build up interesting fillings. Remember that this stitch is also used in smocking, and the gathers used in smocking suggest ringed stem stitch (10), which is actually 2 rows of alternating stem worked over regularly spaced bars of satin stitch.

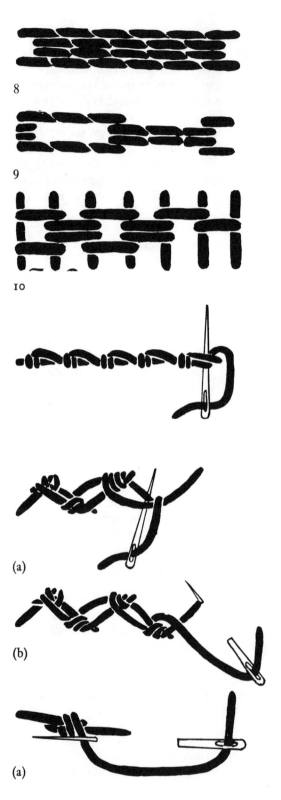

8

9

10

11 *Portuguese Stem* is a development of simple stem stitch. Begin with a stem stitch and then whip it twice, drawing the second coil below the first, make another stitch, keeping the thread at the right side of the needle, and bring the needle to the surface at the top of the preceding stitch. Whip both the top of the first stitch and the bottom of the second as shown in the diagram, and repeat to the end of the row. This stitch can be developed into:

12a and b *Zigzag Portuguese Stem* Work as for straight Portuguese Stem, but remember to work the stem stitches in a zigzag fashion before whipping the two ends together.

(a)

(b)

13a and b *Looped Portuguese Stem* is similar to whipped buttonhole stitch worked vertically. The ends of the stitches are whipped twice, but place the second one above the first, and pick up a tiny piece of material with the first one, to prevent the stitch rolling over.

(a)

18

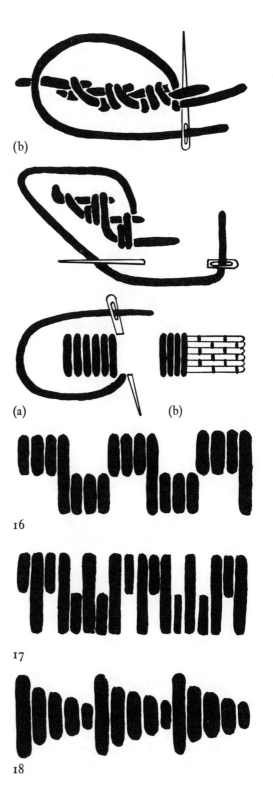

(b)

14 This stitch when worked diagonally is ideal for drawn fabric embroidery. Simply leave 2 threads of the fabric between each pair of buttonhole stitches and make each stitch 4 threads deep.

15a and b *Satin Stitch* For a really smooth, satiny effect, this stitch should be worked with only one thread, no matter how fine, and, where it is possible, pad it either with stitches or some firm fabric such as thin card or leather.

(a)   (b)

16, 17, and 18 show the development of simple satin stitch into borders. For the best results these borders should be worked true to the thread of the fabric.

16

17

18

19, 20, and 21 take these stitches to the stage where it is possible to use them as fillings for linen embroideries, drawn ground, canvas and net work. For linen and canvas work a soft, spreading thread will probably give the best results. For drawn ground a hard round thread no thicker than the threads of the background is ideal. Net embroidery usually requires fine linen lace thread or fine, tightly twisted silk or cotton threads, which give lovely, lacy effects. For closer and glossy fillings, floss silks are admirable.

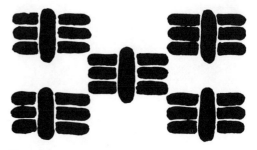

19

20

21

22 *Roumanian Stitch* is a development of satin stitch.

23 *Threaded Roumanian Stitch* The stitches should be worked in groups of any desired number with a fine round thread and a coarse but soft one should be slotted with a blunt-ended needle, which is called a tapestry needle, under the blocks along the upper and lower edges.

24 A suggestion for a filling stitch.

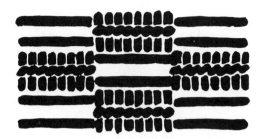

25 *Zigzag Roumanian*

26 *Encroaching Roumanian*

Both these stitches look attractive on canvas 26 is particularly good for embroidered rugs, as it shows to advantage when it is worked with a very coarse thread, and it gives a pleasant ribbed effect.

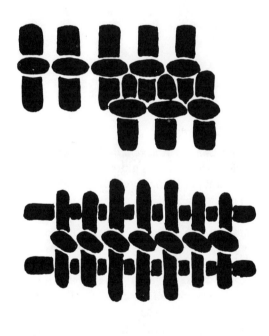

27 Another way in which Roumanian stitch can be threaded. Do use a different weight of thread for the interlacing.

28 Roumanian worked with coarse thread and overstitched with a Roumanian worked with a finer thread.

29a and b *Plaited Roumanian* is a handsome band stitch which shows to advantage when it is worked with a coarse thread. Begin by making a Roumanian stitch which is tied on the left instead of in the centre. Now take the needle back to A and make a second stitch over, and as long as, the first one AB. Bring the needle out at C, tie the new stitch down, and take the needle through the fabric and bring it up at D. Repeat the first and second stages alternately.

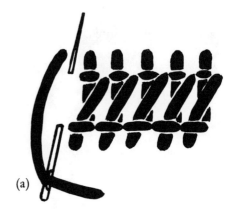

(a)

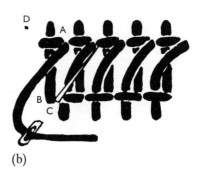

(b)

30a and b *Chained Roumanian* This stitch looks effective on canvas, or as a drawn ground stitch, and as a band, or filling stitch. It is worked from left to right. Begin by making 2 Roumanian stitches a little distance apart but with the tying dots touching. Now make a third stitch exactly as long as, but between, the first 2 stitches, working horizontally. All the points should meet. The diagram shows quite clearly how to fit in the next pair of stitches. Repeat the sequence to the end of the line.

(a)

(b)

31a and b *Crossed Roumanian*

(a) Begin by making a slanting stitch AB, bringing the needle out at C.

(b) Halfway up AB make a stitch CD, bringing the needle out at E. Take the needle back into the fabric at D and begin again at F.

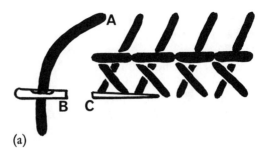

(a)

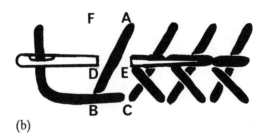

(b)

32 *Roumanian Border* This is a broad border which is composed of simple and threaded Roumanian stitch. Work it as is clearly shown in the diagram. One row of fairly wide simple Roumanian, with a row of quite wide interlocking Roumanian on each side of it. Interlace the outer edges only with a thick thread.

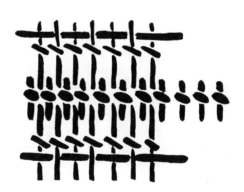

33 *Double Roumanian* Begin by making the stitch AB, and bring the needle out at C. Make a small, straight stitch, CD, and take the needle through the ground to E. Insert the needle at F and bring it out at G. Make a stitch GH and bring the needle out at I.

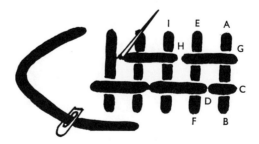

34a and b *Chinese Stitch* looks best when it is worked as a drawn ground band or filling stitch on loosely woven linen. It is based on satin stitch and is extremely simple to work. Make one stitch AB over 6 threads, take the needle to C, 2 threads below and 2 threads to the left of B. Work CD over 4 threads. Pass to E, 2 threads below C, and make the stitch EF over 4 threads. Take the needle back to D and make stitch DG over 6 threads. Now follow the diagram. The second diagram shows 3 rows, AB and C arranged as a filling. When this stitch is worked on a linen scrim the loose threads of the fabric are pulled apart in a most interesting manner.

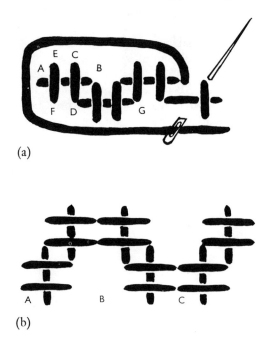

(a)

(b)

35a and b *Butterfly Stitch* Begin at A and make 3 satin stitches, ending at B. Pass the needle through the fabric and bring it out at C, in the middle of and just above the first stitch. Pass the needle upwards, under the satin stitches D, over the thread and downwards under the stitches, as at E. Insert the needle at F, bring it out at G, and repeat to the end of the row.

(a)

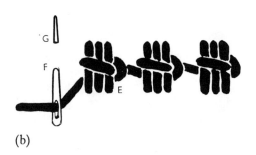

(b)

36a, b and c *Fishbone Stitch* is yet another development of satin stitch. (b) the open method in which the stitches are worked fairly wide apart over a central band. For added interest work a row of close, coarse satin stitches in place of the central thread, and over it work open fishbone with a fine thread, and make the fishbone wider than the satin band. (c) shows how interesting this stitch becomes when it is worked in an irregular manner. It is very lacy when a fine thread is used.

(a)

(b)

(c)

37 *Corded Fishbone* Work 2 fairly widely spaced rows of stitches such as stem, chain or back, and over them place a row of fishbone stitch.

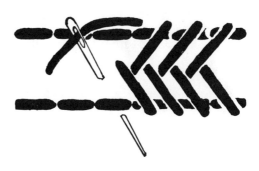

38 *Herringbone Stitch* (a), (b) and (c) show how herringbone stitch can be developed from a simple form to a more complex one. (d) and (e) show two ways in which the herringbone group of stitches may be threaded. The best results are obtained when the top stitchery is the same thickness as, or a little coarser than, the lower stitches.

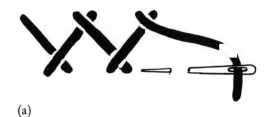

(a)

b—closed herringbone

(b)

c—chevron stitch

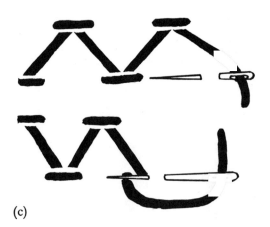

(c)

d and e—threaded herringbone

(d)

(e)

(f) and (g) are filling or border stitches worked with simple herringbone, and are suitable for linen and net embroideries, drawn fabric and canvas work.

(f)

(g) is enriched with darning. The vertical lines of darning should be worked with a fine thread, and the horizontal ones with a coarse thread.

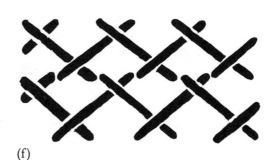

(g)

(h) is a form of tied herringbone which makes a good border stitch. It is possible to work it quite freely, but it is also attractive when worked on the counted thread. Bring the needle out on the lower edge of the border at A. Move 6 threads across and 8 threads up, then pick up 2 threads. From the point at which the needle emerged move 4 threads down and 2 threads back, then pick up 2 threads. From this point move down 12 threads, 2 back and pick up 2. Repeat to the end of the line. Chevron stitch is similarly adaptable, and several rows of chevron worked in this manner, and enriched with heavy darning, makes either a border or a filling.

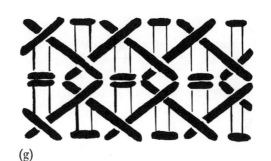

(h)

(i) shows closed herringbone worked in groups of three, with a space between the groups equal to the amount of material picked up for each stitch.

(i)

27

39 *Triple Herringbone* This neat stitch with a raised effect is composed of 3 rows of plain herringbone, each row a little shorter than, and on top of, the last one. The diagram shows the method quite clearly. As a variation for very coarse work, make the row of triple herringbone really large, and then lace all the 3 rows of stitches together with a thick thread. (b) A second variation. Two rows of herringbone are worked as in the preceding stitch, but the third row is worked over and between them.

(a)

(b)

40 *Paired Herringbone Tied* A row of fairly widely spaced herringbone stitches is worked, and then a second row is placed over and between the stitches of the first row. Back stitch both rows together as shown in the diagram.

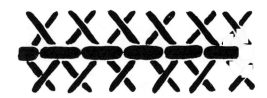

41a and b *Plaited Herringbone* This is a raised band stitch which I found on an English sampler dated 1732. I named the stitch, and then found a drawing of it, under the same name, in a book which was published in 1907. It is easy enough but most people prefer to work this stitch on an openly woven material, in order to count the threads. Bring the needle out at A, move back 6 threads and down 4 and make the stitch AB. Bring the needle out at C, 4 threads below A, move back 8 threads to D, and make the stitch CD. Bring the needle out at E, move 2 threads back from B and make the stitch EF. Bring the needle out at G, 2 threads below C. It will be seen that 6 threads are always picked up, and that every stitch moves backwards 2 threads.

This stitch looks exciting when it is worked over a padding of orange sticks, or thick cane, on a canvas ground.

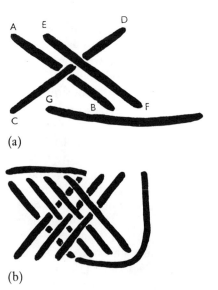

(a)

(b)

42 *Chevron Stitch* The working method is shown in the herringbone group (38c).

(a) is a simple border built up with 2 rows of interlaced chevron. One or two colours may be used. A quite different effect is obtained if the interlacing is omitted.

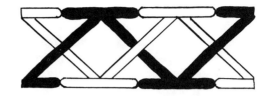

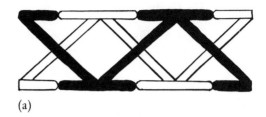

(a)

(b) shows a broad border of chevron stitch enriched with pairs of satin stitches tied in the centre.

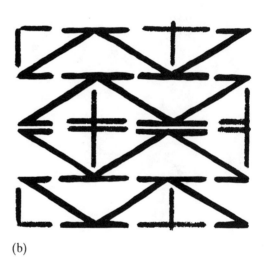

(b)

(c) An even wider border, in which the chevrons should be worked with a finer thread than the 2 centre rows of threading. The method of interlacing the centre rows is shown in the herringbone diagrams. Large french knots complete the border. Both (b) and (c) are effective as fillings.

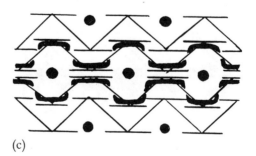

(c)

29

43a shows a motif built up with chevron stitch, which is suitable for linen embroidery, net and drawn fabric. The motif can be used for border or all-over patterns. A bolder effect results from the addition of interlacing, French knots or darning.

For drawn fabric, a small filling in the centre of the motif, such as wave stitch, gives richness and character to the whole. Section A–B is suitable for a border or a motif, and A–C forms yet another border pattern.

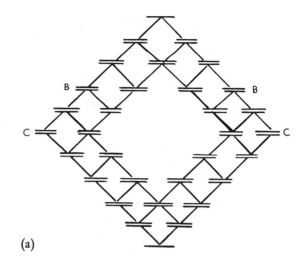

(a)

(b) shows another arrangement of this motif, and (c) is a section of (b).

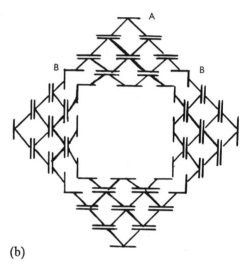

(b)

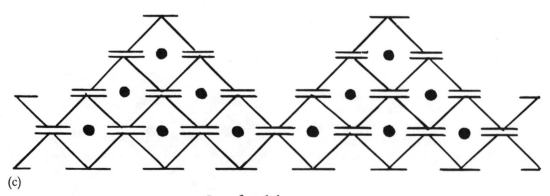

(c)

● french knots

44 shows chevron stitch arranged as a filling, one in which colour could play an important part.

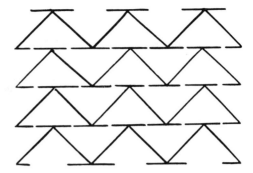

45 *Back Stitch* This easy stitch has unlimited possibilities.

46 *Whipped Back Stitch* Whipping is generally worked with a thread of the same thickness, or somewhat thicker than the thread which was used for the back stitch. An unusual cord-like stitch, similar to one which is often seen in old Japanese embroideries, will be obtained if the back stitch is worked with a fairly soft, thick thread, and the whipping is done with a much finer thread and pulled a little. Closely worked rows of very fine back stitch make a dainty filling for white work.

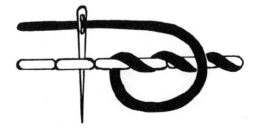

47a Two suggestions for their arrangement. It will be realized that for the second arrangement an even number of threads must be picked up for each stitch.

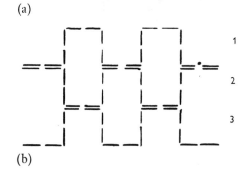

(a)

47b, c, and d, are suggestions for back stitch open fillings. Each stitch in (c) and (d) must be worked over an even number of threads.

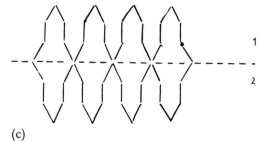

(b)

(c)

(d)

48a, b, c, d, and e show back stitch in other arrangements which look very dainty when each stitch is worked over 2 threads of the fabric. They are suitable for black work and white work. When worked on a large scale with thick thread they are just as attractive.

(a) is the simplest.

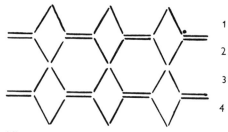

(a)

32

(b) Work the top half of the row of motifs, turn and complete the shapes. In each succeeding row arrange the motifs alternately. When the pattern is complete add the stars and crosses in back stitch.

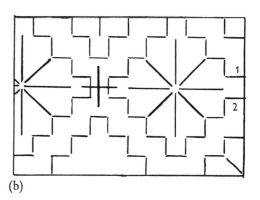

(b)

(c) This attractive filling is worked in the same order as (b). Add the crosses when the pattern is complete.

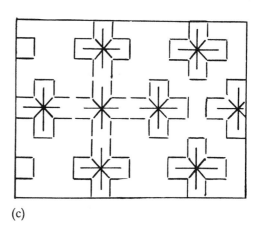

(c)

(d) shows 3 different treatments of the motif (c).

(d)

(e) A simple filling.

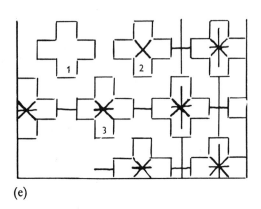

(e)

(f) Work the rows of back stitch as shown at A. Add cross stitches between every pair of rows as at B. Complete the filling with 4 couched lines in the centre of each unit, as shown at C.

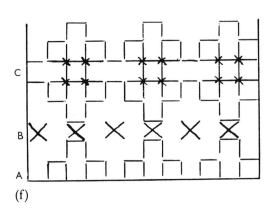

(f)

(g) Another easy-to-follow filling which is worked in stages similar to (b).

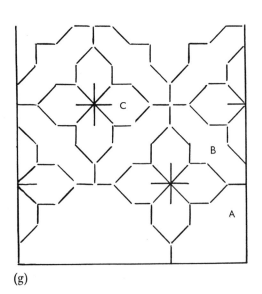

(g)

34

(h) Work rows of embattled back stitch as shown at (a) and complete the filling with rows of running stitch.

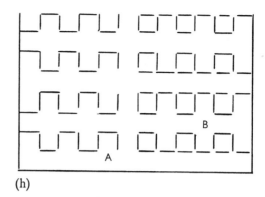

(h)

49 *Zigzag Whipped Back* Work 3 rows of back stitch with a small space between them. Begin from the right at A, and whip the bottom and middle stitches together, bringing out the needle at B. Do not pierce the fabric. Now whip B only. Repeat this process, alternately whipping 2 stitches, and then 1, to the end of the row.

50 *Double Pekinese* is a simple variation of Pekinese stitch yet it looks very different. Work 2 rows of back stitch close together and then thread it. The Chinese used fine gold for the second stage of this stitch, and often filled quite large shapes with closely packed rows.

51a and b *Running Stitch* can be developed into attractive fillings, and in this form it is usually known as darning. All the fillings suggested here look delightful when they are used to fill a shape either partially or completely. Alternatively place these fillings behind a shape, allowing it to touch the outline so that it makes a shadow (58a and b).

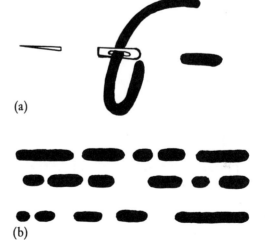

(a)

(b)

35

52 (a) For this pattern darn over 10 threads and under 4, leaving 2 threads between rows 1 and 2. Repeat at 3 and 4, leaving 12 threads between 2 and 3.

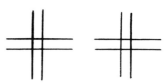

(a)

(b) shows stage 2, when the same pattern is worked vertically.

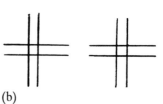

(b)

(c) shows the result when triangles of back stitches are added to the corners of the squares. Work these rows horizontally.

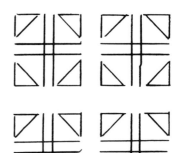

(c)

53 To make this pattern darn over 4 threads and under 4 threads for 3 rows, as shown at stage 1 in the diagram, leaving 1 thread between 2 rows. Leave 4 threads and then repeat until the shape is filled horizontally. Now darn vertically between the blocks as at 2A, working over 4 and under 2 threads. Finish with cross stitches 4 threads long and 2 deep as at 2B.

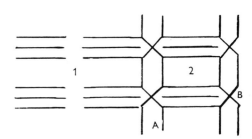

54 This filling is simple but effective. Work over 6 threads and under 2 for 2 rows, then under 6 and over 2 for 1 row. Repeat leaving 1 thread between the rows.

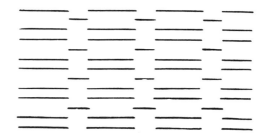

55 Work 4 rows of darning over 4 threads and under 4 threads for 4 rows, leaving 1 thread between rows. Now work a row of cross stitches 4 threads each way. Repeat from the beginning.

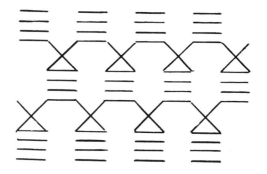

56 Begin at stage 1, darning over 4 threads and under 4. Leave 1 thread between rows and place the stitches and spaces alternately. Complete as shown at stage 2 by darning over and under the stitches without piercing the background.

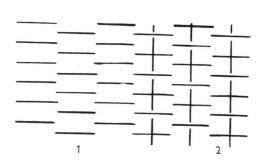

57 Begin at A, darning over and under 2 threads alternately. Leave 10 threads between rows. When the shape is filled work in the opposite direction, beginning between the stitches of the first row, and make squares. Complete with a star shape of satin stitches which meet in the centre of each square, as shown at B.

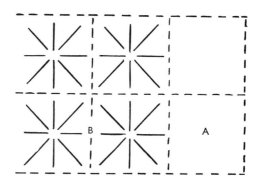

58a *Running Stitch* used to form a shadow behind a shape.

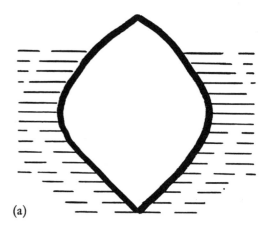

(a)

(b) *Running Stitch* used as a partial filling.

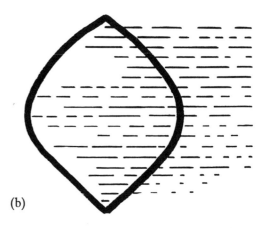

(b)

59a and b *Wing Stitch* Working from left to right make a slanting stitch, as at A, taking care to follow the diagram accurately. The second half of the stitch must be shorter than the first half.

Now take the thread round the stitch without piercing the ground, as at A. Take up the fabric from B to C and repeat.

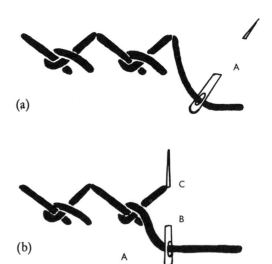

(a)

(b)

60 *Crossed Wing Stitch* is worked exactly like wing stitch, but the last movement brings the thread in front of the last stitch, as shown at B, and the first crossing stitch A is threaded under the second stitch.

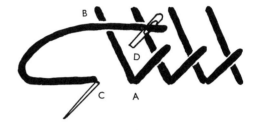

61 *Short Legged Cross* Begin at A and make a diagonal stitch AB. Bring the thread out at C, make a short stitch DC and repeat. This stitch may be used on linen, canvas, net or scrims as a powdering, a line or a filling.

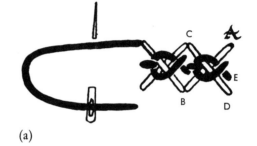

62a and b *Knotted Cross Stitch* This stitch looks best when it is worked with a fairly coarse thread, and it is equally at home on canvas, nets, linens, and silks. Remember that it is not always necessary to count threads, and that this stitch can be used on curved lines. Begin at 1A, and pick up BC. Now pick up DE and the cross stitch is complete. The cross is fastened with a tight twisted chain stitch which does not penetrate the ground.

(a)

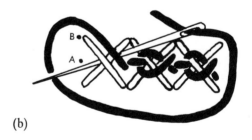

Insert the needle at A and pick up AB. Complete the cross and bring the needle out at A again, in readiness for the next twisted chain.

(b)

63 *Oblong Rice Stitch* Work a foundation of oblong cross stitch, and cross the corners of each one with back stitch.

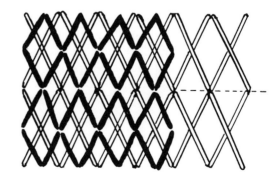

64 *Oblong Smyrna Cross* Make an oblong diagonal cross stitch and work an oblong straight cross over it.

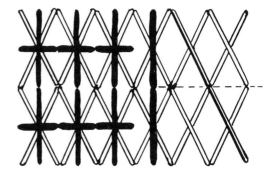

65 *Diagonal Oblong Rice Stitch* Work this stitch diagonally as a half drop.

66 *Diagonal Smyrna Cross* Work as a half drop, diagonally.

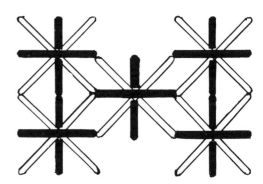

67 *Alternate Smyrna* Arrange the top crossing thread alternately, horizontally and vertically, as shown in the diagram. Although this is such a simple arrangement it alters the appearance of the stitch completely.

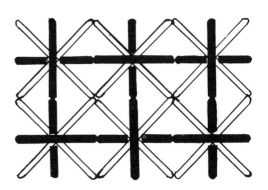

68 *Diamond Oblong Cross* Instead of back stitching the corners of the cross, make 4 buttonhole stitches into the spaces at the sides of the cross. This new arrangement gives a slightly raised effect.

69 *Long Armed Smyrna* Arrange large cross stitches in horizontal rows, but move each row half the width of the stitch to either right or left of the preceding row. Place the horizontal stitches over 2 crosses.

70 *Double Oblong Cross* This stitch was found in a Victorian embroidery book, and was used in Berlin Wool work. Fill a shape with oblong cross stitches, and then work over them with another layer of oblong crosses exactly the same as the first ones but dropped halfway down the stitches in the first layer. This is so durable that it is an ideal stitch for upholstery.

71 *Double Smyrna Cross* and an even more complicated version were both found in the Victorian book mentioned above. Work a cross stitch over 4 or 8 threads according to the size of the canvas, as at 1. Work an oblong cross vertically as at 2, and follow with a horizontal oblong cross, as at 3. On top of all this work a straight cross, and the stitch is complete. Many variations in colour and texture are possible if each section of a filling is completed before the other rows are added. Shades of one colour, or different kinds of thread of the same colour, and contrasting colours, will all give fascinating effects. This stitch is raised and very firm.

Chained Stitches

Simple chain stitch must be one of our oldest decorative stitches, and through the ages, by accident, and sometimes by design, many lovely variations have been discovered. I feel that many more interpretations will be given to us, and eagerly await their advent. For every kind of chain a loop of thread must pass under the needle (72a). Most of the following stitches are variations based on variations, and the first one is called

72a and b *Tied Chain* Work 2 rows of chain close together, and be sure that each row contains the same number of stitches. Re-thread the needle, and bring it out between the rows. Pass it under the inner edges of them. Draw the thread through until only a small loop remains, and then pass the needle through it, from the back. Pull firmly upwards to tighten the knot, and repeat the process to the end of the line.

73 *Threaded Chain* Work a row of simple chain with a medium thread, and interlace it with a coarse one, leaving fairly large loops at each side. Tie the loops with a short stitch worked with a fine thread. Variations of types and weights of thread for this stitch produce surprisingly different effects.

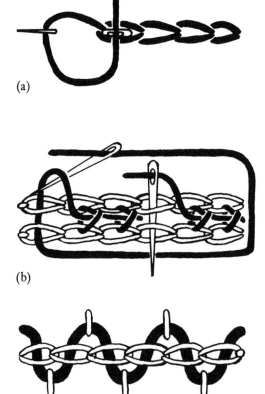

(a)

(b)

42

74 *Crossed Chain* Work 2 rows of chain stitches side by side, and whip the inner edges of the rows together, first from left to right, and then right to left. For a really thick line whip both rows of chain in each direction with a very coarse thread.

75a and b *Broken Chain* is our first really new way of thinking about chain stitch. Make a single chain stitch, then pass the needle through the ground from A to B.

(a)

After pulling the thread to the surface, pass the needle under the bar at the end of the stitch. To complete the chain insert the needle at the side of the bar and make another single chain. Repeat to the end of the row.

(b)

76 *Linked Chain* Begin with a long single chain. Take the needle back, to the middle of it, then from that point make another chain as long as the first one. Take the needle back to the end of the bar which completes the first stitch, as shown in the diagram, and from there make another chain. Repeat.

77 *Shell Chain* Begin at A and make a small chain stitch. From B make another chain twice as long as the first one. Make a small one and a long one, taking the top of each stitch into the same long chain, as shown in the diagram. Repeat.

78 *Waved Chain* is a development of shell chain. Begin with a small chain, and then make 2 more chains, each a little longer than, and to the right of, the first one. Now work leftwards, fitting all the new stitches into the end of the longest one, as shown in the diagram. Continue working backwards and forwards alternately.

79 *Picot Chain* Make a chain stitch, then pass the the needle under the right edge of it, and pull the thread gently through. Insert the needle under the thread and inside the stitch and repeat.

80 *Barred Chain* This is a simple arrangement of alternate chain and twisted chain stitches.

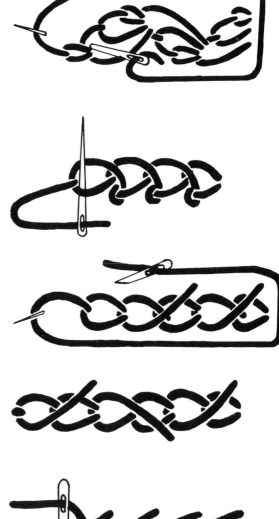

81 *Alternating Barred Chain* is a development of barred chain. Zigzag the twisted chain stitches.

82 *Centre Chain* Begin by making a fairly long chain stitch, and place a fly stitch round it. Take the needle inside the chain to A in the diagram and repeat the chain and fly stitches alternately.

83 *Triple Chain* Work this in the same way as centre chain, except that 2 little chain stitches are worked instead of the fly stitch.

84 *Raised Chain* First work a row of little chain stitches. With the needle inside the first stitch begin to work a second row on top of the first one, but make each stitch twice as long as those in the under row.

85 *Petty Chain* is composed of alternate feather and chain stitches. The feather must be looped into the chains, and worked close beside them. This stitch was made by a student who misunderstood the working of alternating barred chain, and it is named after her.

86 *Open Raised Band* This filling stitch is a variation of raised chain band, and it fits easily into all kinds of shapes. It can be worked in several ways, each of which gives a totally different result. First place evenly spaced satin stitch bars across the shape to be filled. A frame is essential here, especially if the shape is wide. Now work openly spaced rows of raised chain, as shown at B, taking care not to pierce the ground. For the first movement take the needle upwards under the one bar, and pull the thread to the left. Make a chain by passing the needle under the same bar from the right, and over the thread, as shown at C. Pull gently and firmly, then repeat the movements on each bar. The following are variations:

a For a solid, knotted filling, pack the rows of chain stitches close together. If desired, shade the filling, or alter the weights of the threads in each row.

b Work open rows of chain, but stitch up and down the bars alternately.

c For a narrow band work a row of chain along each edge of the bars, and leave the centre exposed.

d For a honeycomb effect, work over two bars instead of one, and in each alternate row begin by working over the first bar only, and then proceed to work over two bars.

87 *Double Chain Band* Make a border of evenly spaced satin stitches, not very far apart. Then work raised chain band over pairs of the bars.

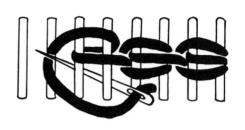

88 *Threaded Open Chain* The bars of this stitch can be used as the foundation for many raised stitches, such as raised stem, Portuguese border and raised chain. Alternating stem is shown in the diagram. As an alternative to working on the bars, back stitch over them, and make additions such as whipping or lacing with a coarse thread.

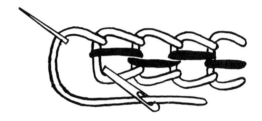

89a and b *Linked Band* is a variation of raised chain band. First make a row of evenly spaced satin stitches, fairly close together. Begin at A and make a link by threading the needle upwards and under 2 satin stitches.

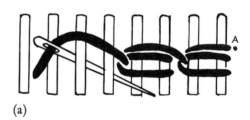

(a)

(b) Pull the thread firmly through and then from the right and downwards make a chain stitch over the same pair of bars. Do not pierce the ground.

(b)

90a, b and c *Zigzag Twisted Chain* is an attractive stitch, which is very useful for covering the edge of appliqué as it does not make a hard line.

(a) The stitch worked in close formation. Bring the needle out at 1 and insert it at 2, and holding the thread with the left thumb so that a loop is formed round the needle. Draw the thread through the loop, and make another stitch, but this time place the thread under and over the left thumb. Work these stitches, alternately facing left and right, to the end of the line.

(a)

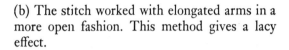

(b) The stitch worked with elongated arms in a more open fashion. This method gives a lacy effect.

(b)

(c) The stitches worked in groups of 3. Vary this number as desired.

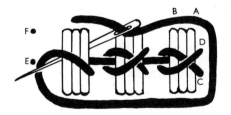

(c)

91 *Triple Twist* is a development of 90 (c). Work the stitches with very long arms, alternating, in groups of 3. Leave a space between groups.

92 *Chained Butterfly* Begin at A and make 3 satin stitches close together and finish at B. From B pass the needle through the fabric to C. Insert the needle at D and pass it under the satin group, making a twisted chain stitch. Pull the thread slightly backwards to tighten the knot and shape the wings of the butterfly. Insert the needle at E, bring it out at F and repeat until the row is complete.

47

93 *Barred Twisted Chain* Work 2 rows of satin stitch bars as shown at A. Over every pair of stitches work twisted chain. Pull the thread slightly backwards as each stitch is made.

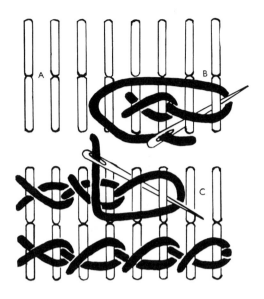

94 *Open Twisted Chain* Work a twisted chain and an open chain side by side.

Now make a reverse twisted chain taking the bar just above the base of the last stitch. Make an open chain into the loop of the first twisted chain, and repeat to the end of the row.

95a and b *Feathered Twisted Chain* Begin with a small twisted chain, then work a feather stitch a little to the right, but on the same level. Make another feather stitch to the right and downwards. Working upwards make another feather stitch, as shown by the needle. Complete the upward movement with a twisted chain on the same level as the feather, but to the left.
Repeat each movement alternately.

(a)

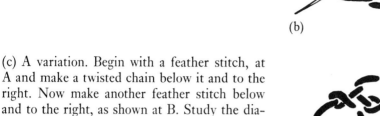

(b)

(c) A variation. Begin with a feather stitch, at A and make a twisted chain below it and to the right. Now make another feather stitch below and to the right, as shown at B. Study the diagram carefully, as the twisted chain stitches are zigzagged.

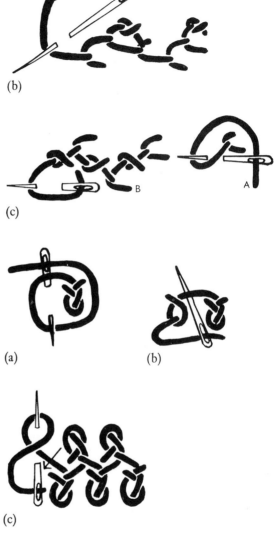

(c)

(a)

(b)

(c)

96a, b and c *Zigzag Rosette Chain* This pretty stitch is a development of rosette chain, which should be mastered first. Rosette chain is simply twisted chain worked sideways, from right to left.

(c) A variation. Make 1 rosette chain in the normal manner, but leave the thread at the top of the stitch. Insert the needle a little to the left of the stitch, point upwards, and loop the thread under the tip. Draw the thread gently upwards, and then pass the needle under the bar which links the two stitches, as shown by the arrow. Do not pierce the ground. Repeat each movement alternately.

97 *Floral Chain* First work a row of rosette chain with a coarse thread, and then with a finer thread add a small chain with a long tail to the end of each stitch. This idea looks equally interesting on zigzag rosette chain.

98 *Double Rosette Chain* Work from right to left. Make a small twisted chain, then insert the needle a little to the left and work a longer twisted chain over the first one. Pass the needle gently under the loop at A, and begin again.

99a, b and c *Tied Ladder* Make a ladder of broad chain stitches. To begin make a chain stitch at A, and pass under the fabric to B and make a second chain. From here pass under the fabric and work a broad chain, as shown at C. Finish the chained border, then begin to work the ladder.

(b) Bring up the needle in the centre of the chain at D, and pass it into E. Repeat until the ladder is finished.

(c) shows that the tying and threading is very like rosette chain. Each pair of threads is tied with a twisted chain, which must not pierce the ground, and then the needle is taken upwards and under 2 threads, over the stitch, and down under the same 2 threads.

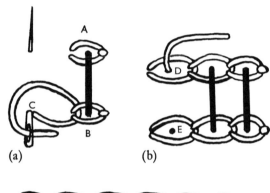

(a)   (b)

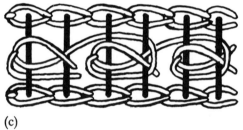

(c)

100 *Lace Border Stitch* Begin at A and make a small twisted chain. Pass to B and make a reverse twisted chain. Thread upwards under the stitches, and make another twisted chain below the first one. Pass upwards under the bar and make a reverse twisted chain on the opposite side. Repeat to the end of the row.

50

101 a and b *Ric-Rac Chain* This exciting stitch looks just like narrow ric-rac braid. First work a row of Spanish knotted feather, which, in spite of the awe-inspiring name, is only a variation of zigzag twisted chain.

Whip the bars together from right to left and left to right, as in crossed chain, and the stitch is complete.

(a)

(b)

102a and b *Crested Chain* To begin, bring the needle up at A, move to the left and slightly downwards, and make a small twisted chain.

Pass the needle under the bar from the top, and make a straight chain, as shown at C. This stitch is capable of many variations, and the ideas given below show how omissions and additions alter its appearance completely.

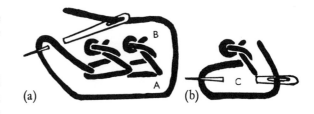

(a)   (b)

103 *Zigzag Crested Chain* Work the stitches alternately from left to right, and do remember to reverse the twisted chain.

104 *Triangular Chain* This simple stitch is crested chain with the second movement omitted, i.e. do not pass the needle under the bar after making the twisted chain.

105 *Interlaced Chain* is worked in a zigzag fashion, and the third movement is omitted.

106 *Reverse Crested Chain* is composed of reversed rosette chain and straight chain.

107 *Buttonholed Twisted Chain* Work a twisted chain on the upper edge and a buttonhole stitch on the lower edge. This stitch looks interesting when it is worked in either a closed or open manner.

108a and b *Portuguese Cable Chain* was found on a piece of old Portuguese embroidery, and I discovered the drawing in a book which was published in 1907. Work as for cable chain by twisting the thread over and under the needle.

Hold the loop on the needle with the right thumb, and make a chain stitch.

(a)

(b) Now pass the needle under the left side of the chain and below the thread, as shown at B, and pull the thread firmly through. Repeat, making every succeeding chain stitch close to the last one.

(b)

109a, b and c *Spiked Knotted Cable* First work a very small twisted chain with a rather long bar. Pass the needle through the bar, making a rosette chain, and complete the stitch with a buttonhole worked as shown in (c). Repeat.

(a)

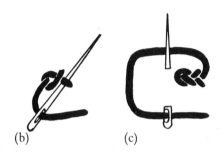

(b) (c)

110 *Knotted Cable and Plain Chain* Work a row of knotted cable chain, which is just like spiked knotted cable except that the buttonhole stitch is made into a chain which encircles the knot. When the row is finished, take a finer thread and work simple chain with a long tail between, and on each side of, the stitches in the first row.

111a and b *Wheatear Stitch* Wheatear is easy to work, and numerous variations are possible. Make two slanting satin stitches for the ears, then bring the needle out the length of a chain stitch below them. Thread under the ears, and complete the stitch by taking the needle to the back of the work in exactly the same place as it emerged. For each succeeding chain, thread under the ears and over the preceding chain. (b) By omitting the ears at regular intervals, a new stitch is produced.

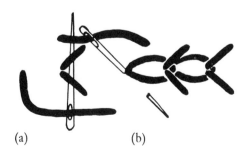

(a) (b)

112a and b *Wheatear and Broad Chain* From the
line stitch we can develop a pleasant filling,
which can be further developed by reversing the
direction of the rows of stitches. With both of
these fillings it is fun to change both the colour
and the weight of the thread in alternate rows.
Other arrangements are equally interesting.

(a)

(b)

113 *Zigzag Wheatear* This stitch is worked
exactly like wheatear, but the stitches are placed
at right angles to each other.

114 *Double Wheatear* Repeat the first movement,
making double ears, and complete the stitch.

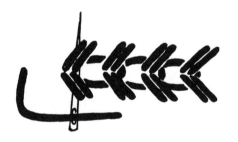

115 *Chevron Wheatear* This is a simple development of double wheatear. The second pair of
stitches must be longer and flatter than the first
pair.

54

116 *Fan Stitch* Work 3 pairs of satin stitches, each pair longer and flatter than the preceding pair, and join them with a single stitch instead of a chain stitch.

117 *Chained Wheatear* Begin by making one complete wheatear stitch. Take the needle to A and thread through the ears returning to A to complete the stitch. Repeat.

118 *Plaited Wheatear* Make a complete wheatear stitch, then work a second chain, beginning only just below the first row. Repeat, but remember to interlace each second chain as is shown in the diagram. This interlacing will raise the first chain and depress the second one.

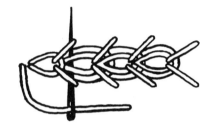

119 *Undulating Wheatear* Work as for simple wheatear, but begin with a pair of long satin stitches and gradually reduce the length of each pair until 3 pairs have been worked. Begin again with a long pair. Alternatively, slowly decrease the size of the pairs to the minimum, then slowly increase to the maximum size.

120 *Double Chain* consists of 2 rows of linked chain worked side by side.

121 *Tied Double Chain* Work 1 fairly large chain, and a small one at right angles to it. Tie this last stitch like a detached chain, and bring the needle up inside it. Make another large chain, as shown in the diagram, and repeat to the end of the line.

122 *Zigzag Tied Chain* is worked like tied chain, but the small stitches are placed on both sides of the large ones.

123 *Whipped Double Chain* This is double chain with the outer edge of each alternate stitch whipped 3 or 4 times.

124 *Linked Double Chain* Work 1 pair of chain stitches side by side, and link them with a twisted chain. The next pair of chain stitches are worked into the base of the twisted chain. Repeat.

125 *Crested Double Chain* Work double chain, adding a whipped buttonhole stitch to each pair of chains.

56

126 *Alternating Double Chain* Work a very small chain stitch, and beside it place another chain 3 times as long. From the end of the long stitch work a short one, and beside it, a long one. Repeat.

127 *Rabbit Eared Chain* Work 2 twisted chain stitches side by side. Link them with 1 open chain worked from right to left. Now work another pair of twisted chain stitches, linking the second one with the open chain. Repeat.

128 *Crossed Double Chain* looks lovely and is not difficult to work. Begin with a small chain, and cross it with a twisted chain placed at right angles to it. Make sure that the cross bar extends to the beginning of the first stitch. Make a second plain chain straight along the line, and cross it with a twisted chain set at right angles to it. Continue in this fashion to the end of the line.

Looped Stitches

Most looped stitches are developments of simple buttonhole stitch, no matter how complicated they appear to be. It follows that plain buttonhole (129) should be mastered before the more advanced forms are attempted.

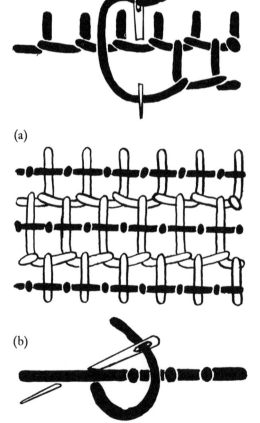

(a)

(b)

130a and b *Buttonhole Filling* This filling is most effective when a fairly coarse thread is used for the buttonhole base, and a much finer, round thread is used for the couching. To begin, work a row of evenly spaced buttonhole stitches from left to right. Then work from right to left, fitting the stitches between those of the first row (129). Complete the filling by working from the left and the right alternately. Now take a fine thread, of a different colour if desired, and beginning from the top left, place it across the centre of the first row of buttonhole stitches. Bring the needle out just below this thread and a little to the left. Make a tiny stitch over the line, and work in this way, putting 1 couching stitch between the buttonholes, to the end of the row. Repeat until all the rows of buttonhole have been covered with this stitch, which is called Bokhara Couching. (130b)

58

131a and b *Raised Buttonhole Band* First make a band of evenly spaced satin stitches, not too far apart. Along the lower edge of this band work a row of buttonhole stitches which do not pierce the fabric. Make the stitches firm but not tight. Finish with another row of buttonhole along the upper edge of the band, worked from the same end but with a reverse movement.

(a)

(b)

132 *Knotted Buttonhole Band* Work as for raised buttonhole band, but enrich each stitch with a tiny chain, which should be pulled tight so that a firm knot is made. To finish the stitch work another row of knotted buttonhole along the upper edge of the band.

133a and b *Reversed Buttonhole Band* First work a band of satin stitches. Begin at the left on the outside of the first satin stitch, take the needle under it from the right, and keep the thread on the right of the needle. Throw the thread upwards, and pass the needle under the same bar again, from the right and at the top of it. Keep the thread under the needle. Pull firmly and repeat on each bar.

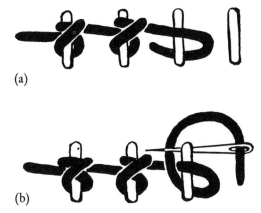

(a)

(b)

59

134a and b *Variations of Reversed Buttonhole Bar*
Two ideas are shown here. (a) simply take the
needle under the bar, and work a firm chain
stitch round it.
(b) the same stitch is worked on a buttonhole
foundation.

(a)

(b)

135a and b *Egyptian Buttonhole* This stitch can
be found on old Egyptian embroidery, and it
looks best when worked on the counted thread.
Make a satin stitch AB, and another one CA. It is
important to make a cross on the back of the
stitch. From A bring the needle out at D.
Buttonhole over bar AB, then buttonhole over
bar CA. Insert the needle at D and bring it out
at E, make a satin stitch EB, and repeat the
movements required for another stitch.

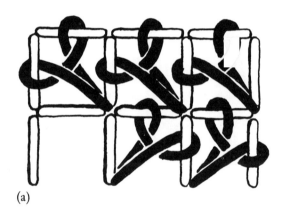

(a)

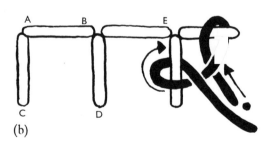

(b)

136a and b *Banded Braid Stitch* This is a broad, lacy border stitch, which was developed from the first buttonhole filling shown in this chapter. Make a straight stitch AB, and bring the needle out at C. Work 2 detached buttonhole stitches on the left side of the bar, taking care not to pierce the ground. Pass to the right side and make 2 more detached buttonholes. Take the needle through the ground at D, and bring it out at E. Now work 1 detached buttonhole between each pair in the previous row. Pass under the fabric from the right to the left side of the border, bring the needle out just below E, and start again with pairs of stitches.
(b) pairs of buttonhole are worked on each side of a single stitch.

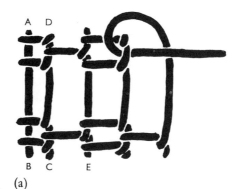

(a)

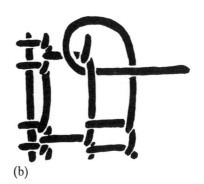

(b)

137 *Up and Down Filling* Although this filling can be worked on almost any fabric, it is particularly interesting when it is used on loosely woven linen as a drawn ground stitch. Work horizontally, taking 3 threads of the fabric on the needle for every stitch. Leave 1 thread between the double stitches, and 3 threads between the pairs. It is quite easy to work backwards and forwards along the rows if the normal buttonhole is always made first.

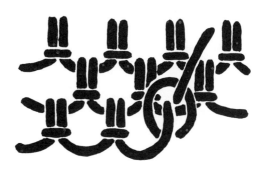

138 *Vandyke Filling* Each stitch is worked on the diagonal of a square of 4 threads. Work a row of Vandyke buttonhole, as shown in the diagram. Invert the fabric, and 4 threads above the last row, begin again. Remember to whip over the base of each pair of stitches in the first row. The tips of the stitches in the third row are made in the same hole as those in the second row.

61

139 *Diagonal Vandyke* Using a unit of 4 threads, work diagonally across the fabric. Invert the work, and make a pair of stitches. Lace through the connecting thread in the previous row, and repeat. The points of the stitches in the third row are taken into the same hole as those in the second row.

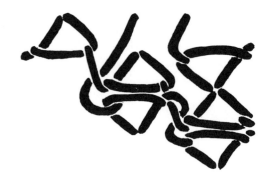

140 *Fancy Diagonal* Using a unit of 4 threads, work pairs of up and down buttonhole diagonally across the fabric. Leave 1 thread between the first and second stitches and 2 threads between the pairs. Interlace the rows, and work the tips of the stitches in the third row into the same holes as those in the second row. *Diagrams 137–40* show fillings which are effective drawn ground stitches, and are equally pleasing on net.

141a and b *Zigzag Buttonhole* This is up and down buttonhole, with the pairs of stitches reversed alternately. Rows of it make a good filling, and it is capable of many variations.

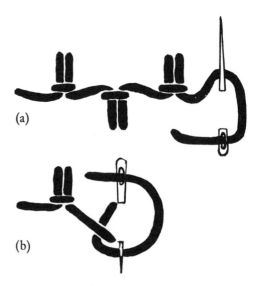

(a)

(b)

142 shows a variation. The second stitch of each pair is much longer than the first one.

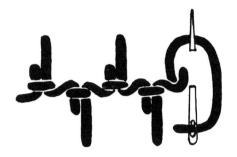

143 *Fancy Ladder* Work a wide border of banded braid stitch (136), with a fairly coarse thread. Interlace the bars with a finer, round thread. With the needle pointing upwards, twist the second bar over the first, and pull the thread firmly through. Repeat this movement to the end of the line.

Feather Stitch is a form of buttonhole, and it presents us with endless possibilities.

144a and b *Plaited Feather* Work a row of feather stitches, leaving fabric between the stitches equal to the length of 1 stitch. Remember to loop the thread under the needle every time a stitch is made.

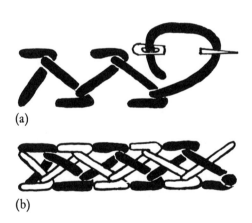

(a)

(b) Work a second row of feather stitches between those in the first row, passing the needle alternately over and under the central threads.

(b)

145 *Raised Feather Band* Take a round thread and lay sufficient bars to fill the border, then, with the same thread work a ladder of evenly spaced satin stitches over them (1 and 2). With a softer, fairly thick thread, work 2 feather stitches on each rung of the ladder (3).

146 *Open Feather Band* The method is exactly the same as for raised feather band, but 1 stitch only is worked on each rung of the ladder. This stitch is lighter in effect and not so highly raised.

147 *Crossed Feather* Work as for plaited feather, but do not interlace the rows. It is interesting to make the second row a little taller than the first one, on one or both sides.

148 *Knotted Feather* Work as for feather stitch, but add a small, firm chain to the bars.

149 *Feather Stitch Filling* This pleasant open filling, which is only of many arrangements of the feather stitch, is explained quite clearly in the diagram. For a raised effect use knotted feather, or lace it in the manner which has been suggested for chevron and herringbone.

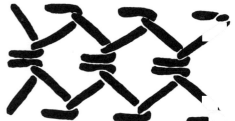

150 *Undulating Feather* Work as for simple feather, but gradually increase the height of the top of the stitches until the maximum has been reached, and then decrease until the stitch is back to its original size. Repeat, this time lengthening the lower edge of the stitches. Work both movements alternately. This stitch can be varied almost indefinitely, and used both as a border and a filling stitch.

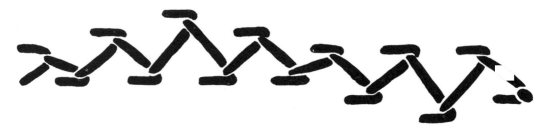

PLATE V

Sampler
Top to bottom:
1 and 2 Chinese stitch
3 and 4 Wing stitch and crossed wing
5, 6, 7, and 8 variations of satin stitch
Lower fringe: Three sided hem
Side fringe : Cross stitch edge

PLATE VI

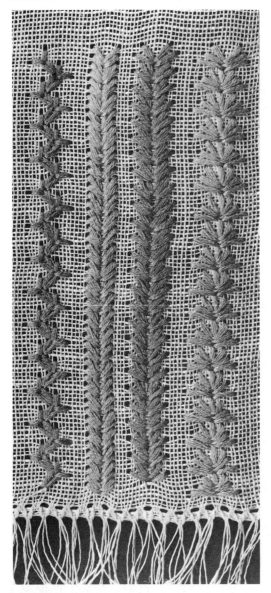

Sampler
Left to right:
    Alternating wheatear
    Double wheatear
    Chevron wheatear
    Fan stitch

Sampler
Top:
    Zigzag whipped back stitch
    Barred zigzag chain
    Barred loop
    Corded fishbone
    Double Pekinese
Left to right:
    Plaited fly stitch
    Plaited Roumanian
    Double fly
    Roumanian border
    Chained fly
    6 and 8 Fly and back stitch border, whipped
    Reversed fly

PLATE VII

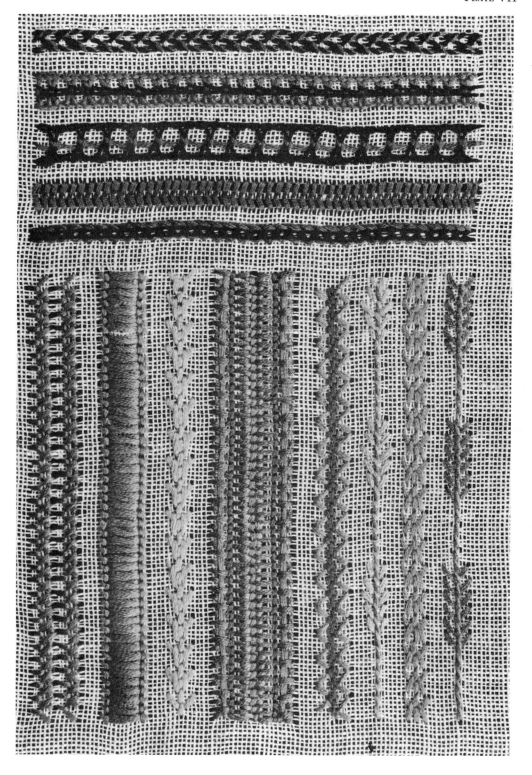

PLATE VIII

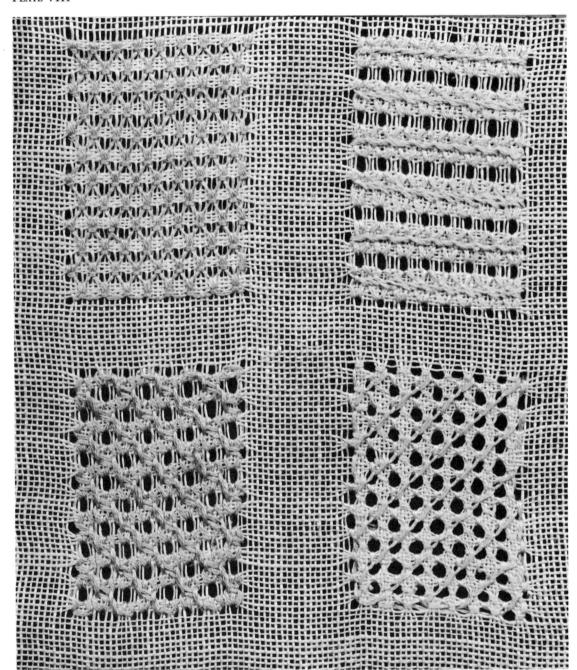

Sampler
Left: Up and down filling
Right: Vandyke fillings
Left: Diagonal Vandyke
Right: Diagonal Vandyke variation

PLATE IX

Part of a box by Catherine Steele, showing drawn
threads held in position with sequins and beads

PLATE X

'Poppy' showing background treated with appliqué
and uneven couched fillings

PLATE XI

'Rose' showing seeded background, surface satin under couched fillings, slipped outlines and uneven fillings

PLATE XII

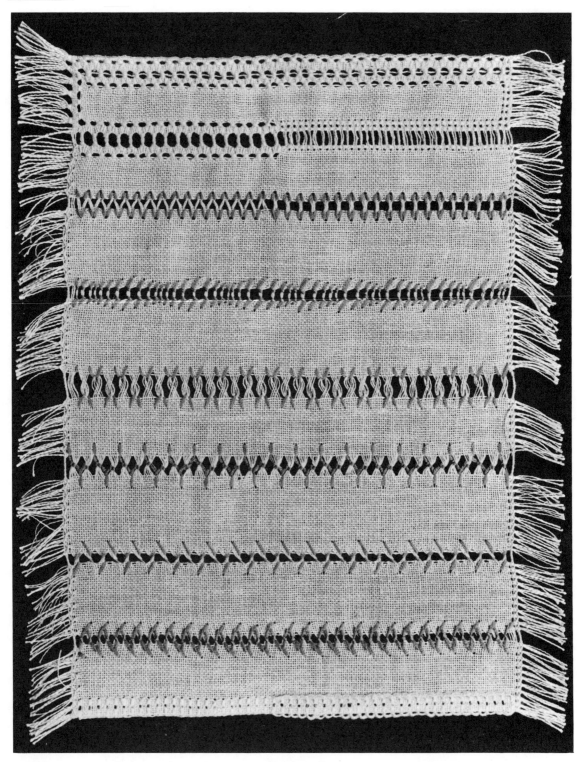

Sampler
Top edge: Buttonholed three-side hem
Row 1 Left: Three-sided hem
         Right: Double dot and single dot
Row 2 Left: Serpentine arrow head hem
         Right: Arrow head hem

Row 3 Undulating hem
Row 4 Chevron hem
Row 5 Looped hem
Row 6 Whipped hem
Row 7 Chained hem

Lower edge:
Up and down edge, the second half
enriched with buttonhole
Fringed side edges

PLATE XIII

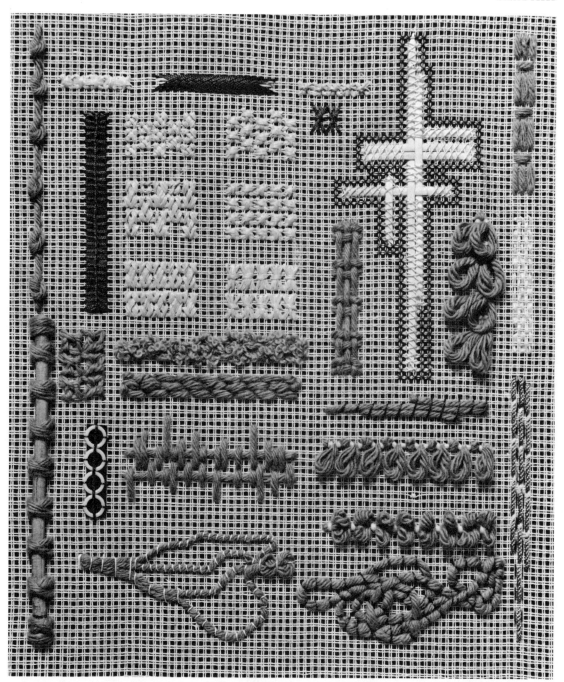

Sampler worked on thrums canvas
Left to right:
    Long armed Smyrna cross
    Plaited herringbone
    Alternate Smyrna
    Diagonal rice stitch
    Diagonal Smyrna
    Diagonal oblong rice stitch
    Oblong rice

Oblong Smyrna
Egyptian buttonhole
Underside couching with 'poodle' wool
Underside couching with rug wool
Woven couching
Flat cane and herringbone stitch
Vertical pendant couching
Staggered couching
Irregular couching

Horizontal pendant couching
Parted couching
Looped couching
Serpentine couching
Left: Knotted couching
    Couched handle cane
Right: Darning on canvas with
    wool, raffia and rayon cord

PLATE XIV

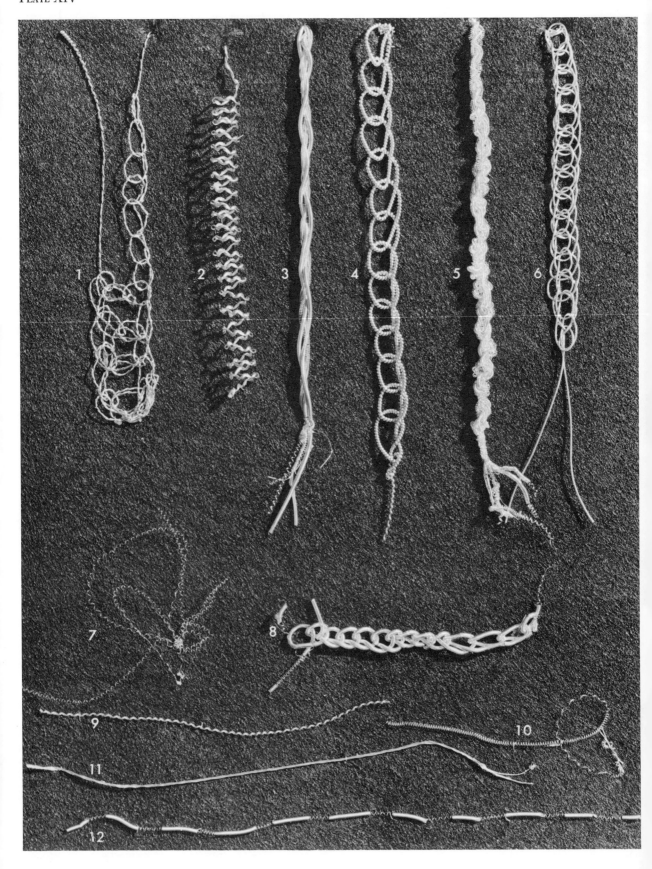

PLATE XV

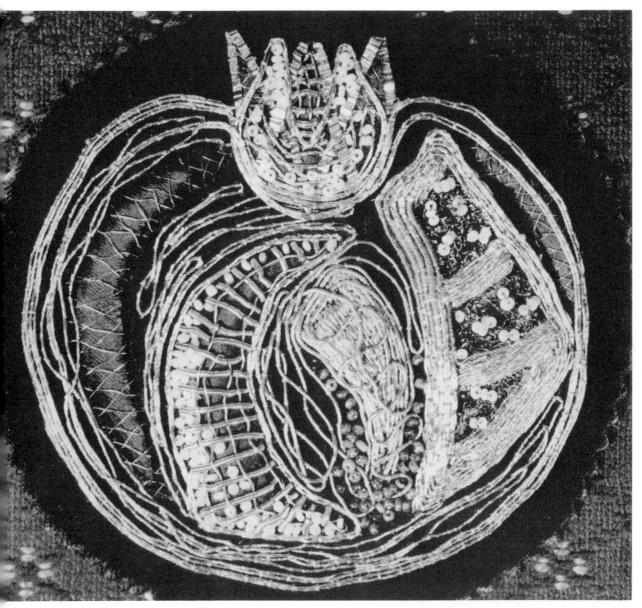

'Pomegranate' by Mary Bunyan, worked with gold
purls, Japanese gold and plate

Gold purls
  1 Pearl purl opened and crocheted
  2 Pearl purl opened and wound on a knitting needle
  3 Smooth and rough purl plaited
  4 Pearl purl crocheted
  5 Smooth purl corded
  6 Passing crocheted
  7 Opened passing
  8 Crocheted purl
  9 Opened pearl purl
  10 Opened purl
  11 Corded passing
  12 Beaded purl

PLATE XVI

PLATE XVII

'Head of Christ' worked with rug, knitting and embroidery wools, tow, Lurex and raffia on rug canvas

'Gabriel' worked on rug canvas. Note the stitching on top of other stitchery

PLATE XVIII

Sampler by Catherine Steele. Darning with strips
of cloth on rug canvas

PLATE XIX

Chinese robe worked with gold thread throughout.
None of the ends is on the wrong side

PLATE XX

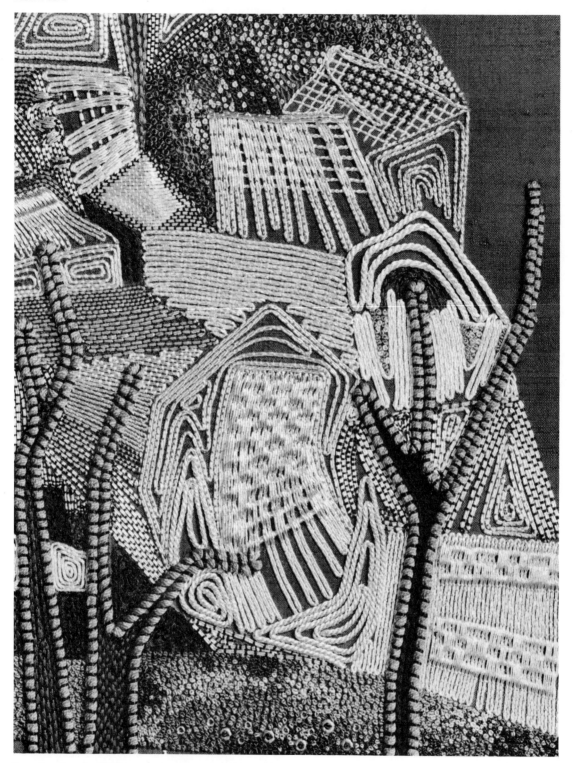

Sampler showing different treatments of gold basket
work and flat gold fillings

151 *Alternating Feather* Work from right to left, and beginning at the top edge of the band, work 2 feather stitches diagonally downwards. Pass to the top, again diagonally, and make 1 feather stitch. Repeat the movements alternately.

152 *Heavy Feather* Begin as for alternating feather, then make a slanting chain stitch from the bottom of the row to the top. Repeat each movement alternately.

153 *Coolie Feather* Begin as above, but end the row with a long buttonhole stitch worked at right angles to the last stitch. Work 2 feather stitches diagonally upwards. Repeat alternately.

154 *Egyptian Feather* Work 2 feather stitches diagonally downwards, then pass to the top of the row and work a small twisted chain stitch. Pass the needle under the bar, and repeat from the beginning.

155 *Triangular Feather* Begin as above, then pass to the top of the row and work a long, straight feather stitch from the inside of the last top stitch. Repeat.

156 *Reversed Feather* Begin as above, then pass to the lower edge of the row and work 1 feather stitch backwards. Thread the needle under the bar, and repeat.

157 *Looped Feather* Make a single feather stitch A, and pass the needle under the bar as shown at B. Repeat.

158 *Inverted Feather* Make a single feather stitch A. Pass the thread carefully under the bar and make the stitch BC. At D the thread is shown in position for the next stitch, which should just meet, but not enter, the stitch on the lower line.

159 *Spiked Feather* Make a single feather stitch AB, and take the thread back to C, so that CD equals BD. Bring the needle through the fabric at D, and make another feather EF. Repeat.

160 *Floral Feather* This is a pretty variation of plain feather. Begin with a single feather stitch, and then make a reverse buttonhole stitch close beside it, as shown at 1. Repeat. A heavier stitch is made by passing the needle under the buttonhole stitches and over the connecting thread, before making another stitch.

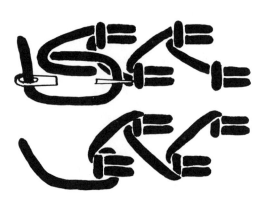

161 *Triple Feather* Work 3 buttonhole stitches, making the centre taller than the outer ones. Work alternately up and down as for single feather. The variation suggested for floral feather works just as well with triple feather.

162 *Reversed Loop Stitch* To begin, bring the needle out at A, and make a horizontal stitch AB. Pick up BC, which is the same length as AB. Loop through AB as shown at D, then move a little to the right, and with the needle pointing upwards pick up another piece of fabric, equal in length to AB. Loop through the last bar, and repeat these movements alternately.

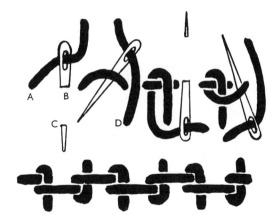

163 *Fly Stitch* is a very simple little loop stitch which is often dotted over a ground in the method called powdering, or used as a line stitch. It is especially useful for fixing appliqué to the ground as it makes a soft edge.

164 *Broad Double Fly* consists of a double row of fly stitches, each linked with the last. Work from left to right, and from right to left, alternately.

165 *Double Fly* Work a rather wide fly stitch with a longer, narrower one over it.

166 *Plaited Fly Filling* is worked in horizontal rows of interlaced stitches. This stitch makes a good drawn fabric filling, and it can be used on net or canvas. It is a useful line stitch too.

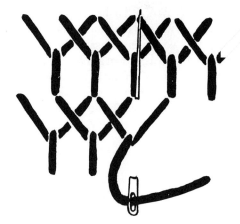

167 *Chained Fly* Work 2 rows of fly stitch back to back, in such a manner that the tails form a row of close bars. Work raised chain stitch over the bars.

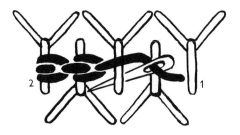

168 *Reversed Fly* Work a fly stitch in the usual manner, then work another one narrower than the first, and upside down and over it. Repeat the movements alternately, making sure that the tails of all the stitches meet down the centre like a row of back stitches.

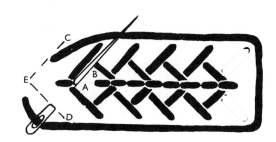

Cretan Stitch is a variation of feather stitch, the only real difference being that the needle is placed obliquely, instead of vertically, for each movement. The stitch may be worked in open or close formation, and it is quite easy to fit it into irregular shapes.

169 *Triple Cretan* Work a row of widely spaced cretan stitches, and over it place 2 more rows, each one beginning a little to the right of the last.

68

170 *Triple Cretan Variation* shows a more interesting arrangement, as each row of stitches is made a little shorter than the last.

171 *Chained Cretan* Begin at A, insert the needle at B, and bring it to the surface at C. Insert again at A, and bring it out at D, as shown in the diagram. Insert the needle at B and work another stitch, then at A, then at B, making 3 cretan stitches on each side. Now work a small open chain stitch with its ends in the middle of the last pair of cretan stitches. Repeat. A round thread is an advantage here, because it allows the background to show between the stitches.

172 *Looped Cretan* Begin at A, insert the needle at B, and bring it to the surface at C. Insert at B again, and bring it to the surface at D. Repeat on alternate sides of the border.

173 *Splayed Cretan* Work one cretan stitch, ABC. Insert the needle at D, below and a short distance outside B, and make a second stitch. At E make a third, even longer stitch. Repeat on alternate sides of the border.

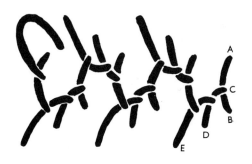

174 *Crossed Cretan* Make a cretan stitch ABC. Insert the needle at D, and bring it out at E, as shown in the diagram. Note that the thread is not looped under the needle. Insert the needle at F, and bring it out at G, without looping the thread. Take the needle to the opposite side of the band, make one cretan stitch, then repeat the movements to complete the crossing.

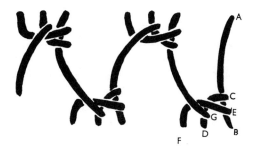

175 *Tied Cretan* Make a cretan stitch ABC, and tie it with a buttonhole stitch, D. Repeat alternately right and left.

176 *Reversed Cretan* Make a cretan stitch ABC. Now make a straight stitch CD, with no loop round the needle, which should emerge at E. Make a straight stitch EF, bringing the needle out at G. Make a long cretan GH, and repeat all the movements to the end of the line.

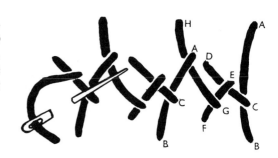

177 *Scotch Cretan* resembles thistle heads. Work 3 straight cretan stitches fairly close together, then pass the needle under the outer edges, upwards and downwards. Pull the thread firm, but not tight. Repeat, leaving a small space between groups of stitches.

178 *Irish Cretan* Begin at A and work 3 cretan stitches, A, B and C, each having the left side much longer than the right side. Now turn the work through a right angle, and make 3 similar stitches just below the plait in the middle of the first group. The short ends of the first stitches should be covered completely. Turn the work again and repeat the first movement, remembering to link the stitches. This stitch looks handsome when it is worked with a round thread, coarse or fine. A stranded thread is not quite as effective.

70

179 *Welsh Cretan* is worked like simple cretan, except that the needle is taken 1 stitch forward with each movement, thus enlarging and raising the plait.

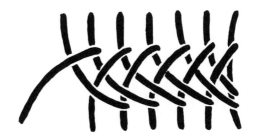

180 *French Cretan* Work a cretan stitch ABC, making BC equal to one-third of the width of the stitch. Now work another one, CD, close to the first stitch. Bring the needle up at E, and make a short stitch BF. Make a small buttonhole stitch, piercing B again. Leave a space between the pairs of stitches on the upper edge when repeating the movements.

181 *Grouped Cretan* is a variation of Scotch cretan. Work 3 stitches with a wide, central plait, and loop them together, pulling the thread quite firmly. Leave exactly the same space between all the stitches.

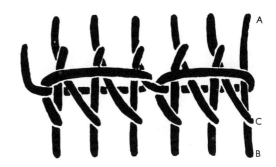

182 *Alternating Cretan* is explained quite clearly in the diagram. Work the stitches close together so that the plait is thick and raised.

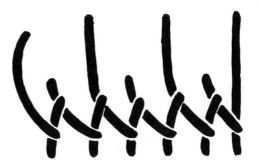

Knotted Stitches

The knotted stitches appear to be so complete that one wonders if any variation from the norm is possible. Old embroidery books, especially those which were first published during the nineteenth century, provide us with a few clues. The Victorian ladies were certainly inventive. Oddly enough the sewing machine provides more clues. Free embroidery worked on a sewing machine holds quite a number of terrors for the beginner, and her lack of control often results in bursts of speed followed by very slow movements. The hesitations, and incorrect tensions, combine to give very lumpy work, which is often condemned by experienced people. Sometimes, however, it is realized that these apparent mistakes have possibilities, and they are eagerly developed into new techniques. One student evolved a delightful filling in this way, and this, in its turn, gave rise to several variations of hand stitches.

Knots give a new character to stitches which have become uninteresting through frequent use. The constant demand for new ideas sometimes results in unintended knots, but even these can be turned to profit, as will be discovered in the chapter on couching.

183 *French Knot* can be worked either in the hand or a frame, but for a really tight, well-shaped knot, a frame is essential. Bring the needle out at A and, holding the thread loosely under the left thumb, twist the needle once or twice round it. Still holding the thread, turn the needle with the twist upon it, to B, and gently insert it into the material. Pull all the thread carefully through, and do not release the left thumb until the last minute. The knot should be round and firm.

184 *Rayed Knot* Make a french knot with a really thick thread and then work long straight stitches, of uneven length, from the outside to the centre of it, with a fine thread.

185 *Spider Knot* Work a french knot with a very thick thread. Take a much finer thread, and, beginning well away from the knot, at A, work a long tailed french knot into the centre of the first one. Repeat as often as desired.

186 *Linked French Knot* A drawing of this stitch was found in a nineteenth-century book, and I think it is best to work it without a frame. Carry the thread along the surface of the work, hold it down with the left thumb, and twist the needle once round it. Insert the needle into the material and bring the point to the surface a fraction of an inch forward. Twist the thread twice round the needle, and draw it up until the twist is near the eye of the needle. Pull the thread through. Repeat, leaving a fairly long stitch between knots.

187 *Jacobean Knot* Make a solid filling of large french or bullion knots, then roughen the surface with small french knots worked with a finer thread, and scattered over it. This method can be found in Jacobean crewel work.

188 *Bullion Knot* A round thread is useful for this stitch as it gives the coiled effect which is so necessary. Without it, half the beauty of the stitch is lost. Pick up a piece of fabric as long as the stitch which is to be made, and push the needle well through the ground. Twist the thread firmly, but not tightly, round the needle, until there is a roll long enough to cover the fabric. Hold the twist under the left thumb, and gently draw all the thread through the knot. Turn the knot over to A, and tighten the thread. Once this knot has been mastered, it is not difficult to add it to many other stitches.
The following diagrams show a few of the many ideas which have been developed recently.

189 *Linked Bullion* is our old friend stem stitch, enriched with plump knots. Leave a short space between the stem stitches, wind the thread round the needle as often as is necessary, and carefully turn the knot over before making the next stem stitch.

73

190 *Chained Knot* is simple chain stitch with bullion knots. Work as for chain stitch, but remember to twist the thread several times round the needle before pulling it out of the fabric. Push the knot to the side of the stitch, and insert the needle ready for the next stitch.

191 *Looped Knot* can be varied in lots of ways, because there are so many kinds of buttonhole stitch. This new look version is the simplest buttonhole of all. Do remember to place the left thumb on the twist before drawing the needle out of the fabric.

192 *Twisted Fly Stitch* Follow the diagram for the method of working this very pretty arrangement of bullion knots and fly stitch.

193 *Twisted Knot* Twisted zigzag chain with bullion knots looks expecially lovely when it is worked with a coarse round thread. Follow the diagram, and the directions for the other knotted stitches.

194 *Ringed Knot* is braid stitch in a new dress. Twist the thread several times round the needle before it enters the ground at A. Bring the needle up at B, and pass the thread under it before pulling the needle through the knot.

195a and b *Knotted Vandyke* Bring the needle out at A, and pick up BC. Twist the thread several times round the needle, pull the needle through the knot, and pass it through the fabric from D to E. After making the first complete stitch, thread the needle under the centre of it and every succeeding stitch, instead of passing through the fabric as at BC.

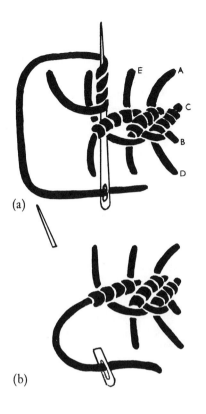

(a)

(b)

196a and b *Fancy Double Knot* Bring the needle out at A, and pick up BC. Draw the thread through and pass the needle under the bar.
(b) Pass the needle under the bar again, and twist the thread several times round it. Pull the knot firmly, and repeat from B.

(a)

(b)

197a and b *Knotted Chevron* Work chevron stitch putting the knot on the second part of the horizontal stitch.
(b) Place the knot in position and pass the needle under it before making the next stitch.

(a)

198 *Chinese Knot* is a stitch which comes half-way between a french and a bullion knot. Thread the needle with several lengths of thread of different colours, pick up a very small piece of fabric, and before pulling the needle through, wind the threads ten or twelve times round it. Hold the twist with the left thumb and gently ease the needle through the knot. Turn the knot into position and pull the threads equally tight. Remember that all knots should be firm. Loose knots are never attractive, as they can be pulled out of shape and tend to move away from their original position.

(b)

199a, b and c *Laced Knot Stitch* Pick up a short piece of fabric. Work the stitches in groups of 3 and leave a short space between groups.

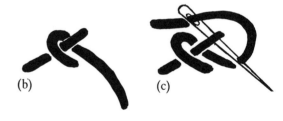

(a)

(b)

(c)

Variations   d — undulated.

(d)

e — tightly packed.

(e)

(f)

f — zigzagged.

200 *Long Armed Double Knot* Work like spaced double knot, but leave the same distance between the stitches, and make them all the same size.

201 *Zigzag Double Knot* is an interesting variation of long armed double knot. Work the stitches alternately above and below the line which is being embroidered.

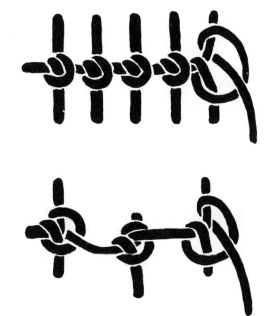

Couching

Couching has been defined as 'to embroider with gold thread, and the like, laid flat'. This is a reasonably good description, but it can be very misleading. Basically, every form of couching is the same, since a thread is placed upon the background and stitched into place in a decorative manner. The thread need not, however, be laid quite flat. It can be looped, knotted and padded, and given extra height in all sorts of ways.

A frame is essential as the background must be really firm and the left hand should be free to guide the thread.

The simplest forms possess the most possibilities, so we will begin with the basic method of couching, and develop it into more exciting forms.

202(a) The thread which is to be couched is brought to the surface of the work after the end has been secured on the back, and held firmly with the left hand. It is sewn into position with small, evenly spaced stitches.

(a)

(b) shows a simple development. The stitches are not spaced evenly and the couching thread must be of a different colour.

(b)

Do remember that braid, cord, wire, leather thongs, cane and metal rods may be couched instead of the usual kinds of threads, but keep suitability for purpose firmly in mind. Wire and metal rods are not particularly charming on cushion covers, but they are effective on hangings and room dividers.

These ideas are not really new. Coloured couching stitches worked over gold thread are to be found in English, European and Far Eastern embroideries. These embroideries are breathtakingly lovely. Braids are to be found on Burmese Kalangas; cords, straw, string and ribbon were used in England from the sixteenth century onwards; and feathers (whole ones and very small) are to be found both on Japanese and Peruvian embroideries. Our own Victorian ladies worked with feathers too. Purists might not call feather work couching, but since feathers are generally oversewn into position with tiny stitches, I have mentioned this idea to give point to my remarks.

(c) The couching stitches are worked with threads of different weights. This method is great fun, and it can be varied in many ways.
Extended Couching (see page 109) Use a medium weight round thread, and couch it with evenly spaced stitches worked with a finer thread of the same colour. This method does help the embroideress to lose the stiffness which is so often associated with couching. The photograph of of *The King* by Doris Warr shows a trial run worked with string (Plate IV).

(c)

203 *Irregular Couching* The length of the couching stitches, and the spaces between them, should be quite uneven. It follows that the thickness of the couching stitches can be varied too.

204 *Crazy Couching* Herringbone worked at different heights, and occasionally tied, is used as a couching stitch. It is only one of many stitches which can be worked in this way.

205 *Serpentine Couching* The thread which is to be couched is wound round the fingers, or shaped in some other way, and literally dropped into the space it is to occupy. It is a good idea to hide the ends, and to assist the thread to fall as desired.

206 *Staggered Couching* Begin to couch a single thread. Add extra ones where greater thickness is desired. This method can be varied in many ways, and it is not impossible to fill shapes with gold thread in this manner.

207 *Parted Couching* This method gives interest to a line which might otherwise look dull, and with care it can be arranged as a filling. Begin to couch a bunch of threads, then gradually open the bunch and display each thread separately. Gradually bring all the threads together again, then couch the bunch until another parting is felt to be necessary.

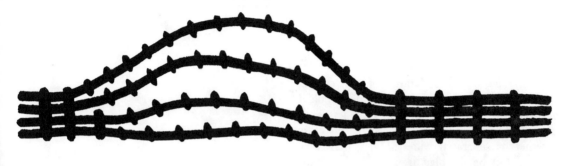

208a and b *Frilled Couching* For a narrow border sew a padding of string, felt, cord or leather along each side of the border (a).

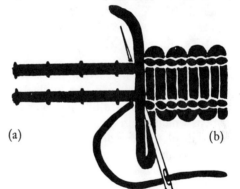

(a)

(b)

(b) Shows the method quite clearly.

(c) shows frilled couching used to give a raised edge to a flat filling. The padding is sewn into position before the filling is worked.

The rows of padding are placed so close together that there is only just enough room for the thread to be couched between them. It will be noted that the couching stitch between the rows of padding is worked on alternate threads only.

(c)

209 *Woven Couching* Fasten 3 round threads at each end of the border they are to fill. Couch them with double rows of weaving. The needle is taken through the fabric at the top of each row, and brought to the surface at the bottom of each row of weaving.

210 *Knotted Couching* Knot a fairly coarse, round thread at regular intervals, and couch it between the knots. The knots may be left loose or pulled tight, and they may be placed close together or separated widely. They may vary in size, and be doubled if necesssary. If this method sounds laborious do remember that it is also effective. It was used both in this and other countries, during the eighteenth century.

211 *Underside Couching* This method dates from the thirteenth century, when it was worked so finely that one can only stare in amazement at the specimens which are in museums, and marvel at the skill of those people who departed from this life so long ago.

Use a fairly soft thread and couch it with a finer but very strong one. Fasten the thread which is to be couched at the right side of the row, and hold the remainder firmly but not tightly with the left hand. The couching thread should be taken up through the fabric, round the top thread, and back through the same hole by which it entered. Pull it firmly until the top thread loops to the back of the work. Repeat at regular intervals. At the end of the row it will be found that the couching thread is running under the fabric in a straight, tight line, and that the top thread is presenting a broken look like back stitch. By varying the position of the couching stitches, and working close rows, many really durable and interesting fillings can be made.

82

This method has many possibilities, some of which are mentioned in the chapter on Canvas Work.

212 *Looped Couching* This pretty stitch is useful for outlines, and although it is quite decorative it is sometimes enriched with beads which are sewn over the couching stitches. Begin with a really thick bunch of threads, and couch it with a fine, strong thread. Make double couching stitches for extra firmness as a single stitch sometimes works loose. Work 2 pairs of couching stitches a short distance apart. Hold the couching thread firmly in the left hand, and with a tapestry needle gently ease the bunch of threads upwards until the required height is obtained. The threads should spread and make a loose ball. Work another pair of couching stitches and again ease the bunch of threads upwards. Repeat to the end of the row.

(a)

213a and b *Horizontal Pendant Couching* This method gives a looped fringed appearance to the thread, and it may be used as a line or as a filling. It is easier to work from below, upwards, if a filling is required. Begin from the right, and holding the thread firmly but not tightly, make 2 couching stitches close together, to hold the end of the thread securely in place. Now loop the thread, using a knitting needle for a gauge, and work another couching stitch as near to the loop as possible. Move a little further leftwards and repeat the process. Continue to the end of the row. If the thread which is being couched tends to slip, or if a single couching stitch does not hold the thread firmly, couch all the way along the line with double stitches worked on top of the other. A variation is shown in (b) Work the rows vertically, and place the couching stitches.

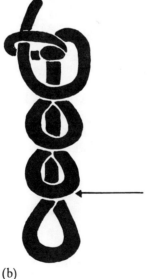

(b)

From simple couching we move on to the very decorative couched fillings, of which there are dozens of well-known ones. Each one can be varied in so many ways that the possibilities are endless. Sometimes a padding of surface satin stitch is worked under a couched filling to give extra colour and weight.

214a *Surface Satin* A thick, soft thread should be used for this padding as it is necessary to cover the ground completely. Any filling which is worked over it should be placed so that the threads do not fall between the rows of satin stitch (b). Many people like to place surface satin at strategic points instead of filling a whole shape with it. Sometimes pieces of fabric are used instead of the padding of surface satin. This method is quick, as the edges of the pieces of material are not turned under, and textured fabrics like hairy tweed and velvet do give interest to the work.

(a)

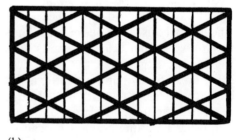

(b)

The couched filling need not fill a shape entirely, and it is not necessary to enclose such a filling with a firm outline. The only requirement is good craftsmanship. Study the photograph of the rose leaves and you will see that this kind of work is very neat (Plate XI).

215a and b Simple net foundation for couched filling.

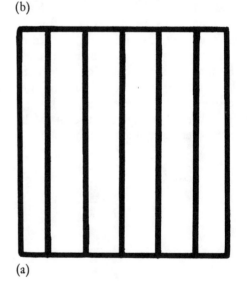

(a)

84

Now let us consider the net, which must be worked before the fillings. The obvious method is to use the same weight and colour of thread for the whole of the net. Certainly, until a beginner has mastered the art of placing her threads evenly, she should not try to do more difficult things.

Having solved this first problem, we find that there are many ways in which the net can be varied.

216a and b shows a simple arrangement of different weights of threads. Change the colour in the middle of (a) only.

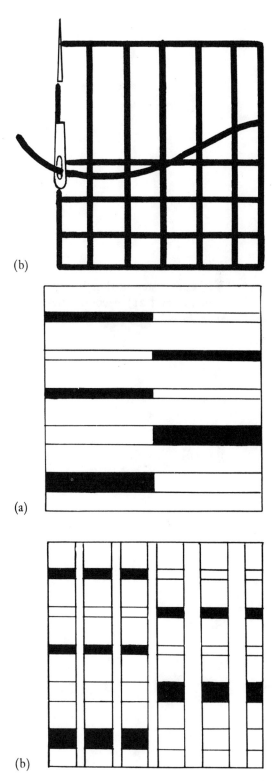

(b)

(a)

(b)

217a and b is a variation of the second method. Change the colour in the middle of (a) only.

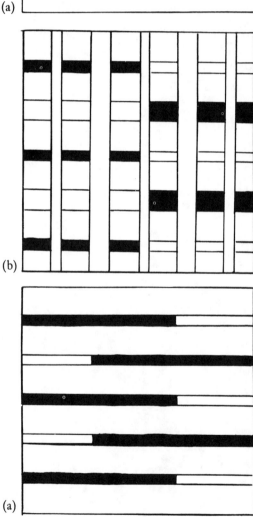

(a)

218a and b takes us a step further, and the hard centre line of 216 and 217 becomes pleasantly loose. Change the colour in (a) only as shown.

(b)

(a)

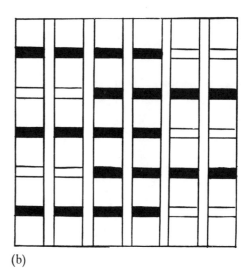

(b)

219a and b shows us that the spaces between the threads need not be even. Do remember that this method is not one for beginners, as it is not easy to work it successfully. Gradually widen the spaces between the rows.

(a)

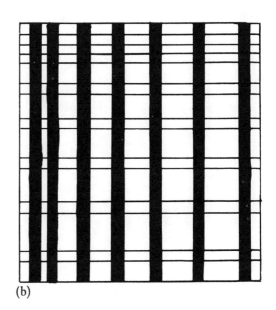

(b)

220 Some couched fillings require two foundations. It is fun to work them with threads of different weights.

(a) worked with a thick thread

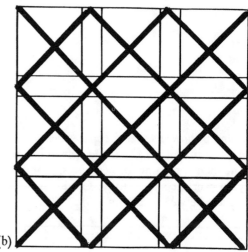

(a)

(b) second foundation worked over (a) with a finer thread.

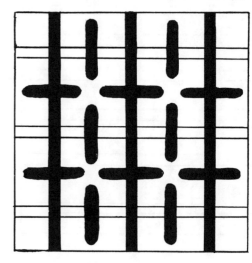

(b)

221 and 222 give ideas for couching the net. When the net is complete, it can be elaborated with other stitches, and a few ways are shown in diagrams 223–7.

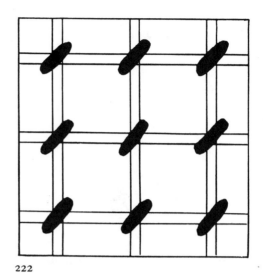

222

It is not necessary to place the top stitchery evenly over the net, and groups of top stitches with spaces between them are often quite effective. Look at the photographs of the poppies and roses on Plates X and XI.

223 Waved filling. Thick pale thread for the net. Lace with a dark thread.

224 Daisy filling. Thick pale thread for the net. Fine dark thread for daisies.

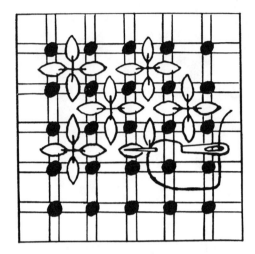

225 Windmill filling. Note double pale threads in the foundation.

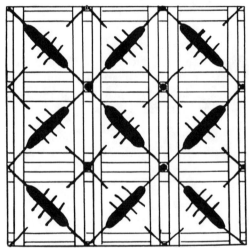

226 Star and lattice filling. Note the irregular spacing of the foundation.

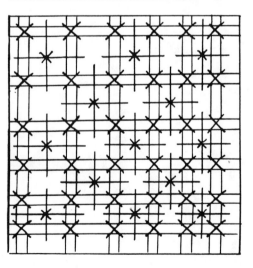

227 Crossed filling. Note the coarse net worked over a fine net.

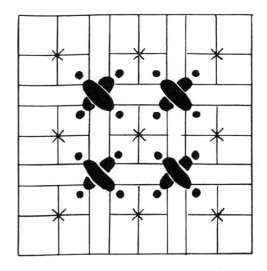

With care it is possible to change the top filling, and use more than one arrangement on a single net.

228 Mixed filling. A shaded effect can be obtained by changing the colours used in the top stitchery, as well as by changing the type and the weight of the threads. Couching is fun, and even now we have not reached the end of the possible variations on this simple theme. Beads, french knots and most powderings may be sprinkled over a filling to link it with another part of the design, or to make it fade gradually away.

Couching with one colour, even the colour of the background, is most attractive and needs no champion. Different weights and textures of threads add interest to this method.

Couching with a number of colours gives the effect of painting, and it is possible to achieve glorious effects in this way.

Remember that gold threads can be used for the basic nets and plate looks particularly good. Fine sewing golds can be used for the top stitchery. Gold threads and woollen ones look very well when they are used together.

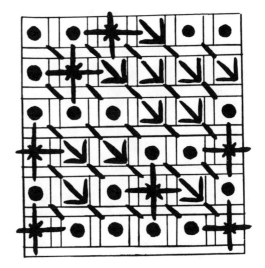

French knots

Satin stitches

Chain stitch

The Sewing Machine Group

It is a joy to the ingenious needlewoman to watch an automatic sewing machine making delightful patterns. So many variations of well-known stitches are suggested by the movements of the machine that once she has started to experiment it is difficult for her to stop. The following diagrams show what can be done with just a few stitches. All of them can be worked freely, or on the counted thread, and most of them can be developed into fillings.

229 *Alternating Buttonhole*

230a and b *Waved Roumanian* Work this stitch in the usual manner but remember to make every sixth stitch much wider than the rest.
An interesting development is shown in (b). The width of the first 5 stitches is gradually increased on one side only, and the knots are worked in a straight line. Repeat.

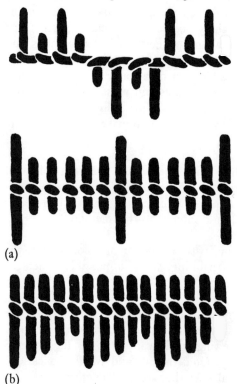

(a)

(b)

231 *Block Cretan*

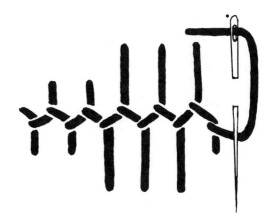

232a, b and c *Closed Herringbone Variations*

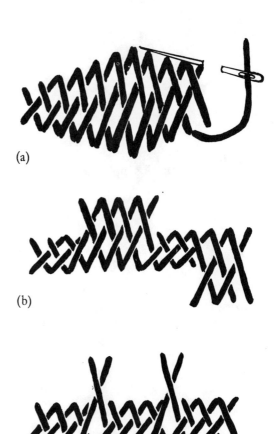

(a)

(b)

(c)

233 *Pagoda Chevron* is worked exactly like simple chevron, except that the thread remains in the same position after the first horizontal stitch is made.

234 *Zigzag Feather* Note that the groups of stitches are placed on a brick formation.

235 *Swinging Feather* can be worked as a single line, as a border composed of 2 rows of stitches, or as a filling.

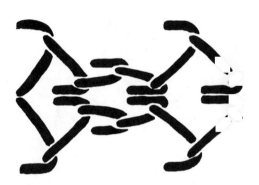

236 *Fly Stitch Garland* is simple and effective.

237 *Arrow Head Fly Stitch* is pretty either as a line or a filling stitch, and it has possibilities as a canvas stitch and a drawn fabric stitch.

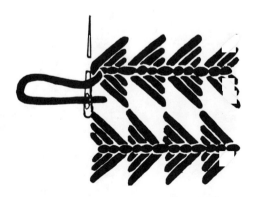

238a, b and c *Zigzag Petal Stitch* (a) Begin with a stem stitch, and from the middle of it work a small chain stitch (b). Take the needle back (c) ready for the next stem stitch. The stem is like alternating stem, and the chain stitches should be worked on each side alternately.

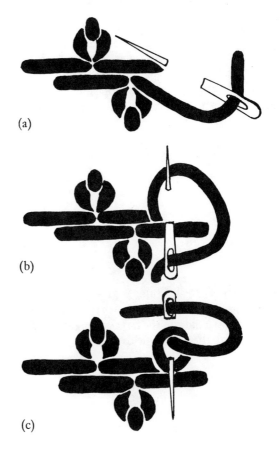

(a)

(b)

(c)

Many edge stitches can be devised after studying the cams which are provided with automatic sewing machines, and these give a refreshingly new look to embroidered household articles. Naturally these edges can be used in a purely decorative manner too, and function can be forgotten.

239a and b *Chevron Hem* is a simple variation of single twist. It is necessary to begin a fair distance from the edge for the V shape to be really effective. Use a bold thread, and begin at the end of the drawn border. With the needle pointing upwards twist the second group of threads, say 4, over the first group. Pull the thread firmly, pass through the fabric 8 threads from the beginning and bring the needle to the surface 8 threads beyond that point.

(b) Repeat, leaving 8 unworked threads between the worked ones. Repeat on the opposite side of the border, using the unworked threads.

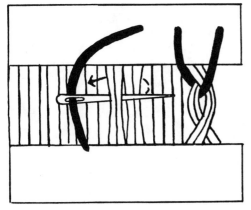

(a)

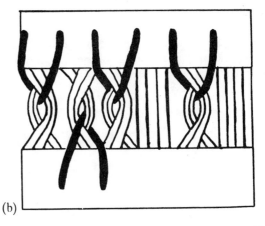

(b)

240 *Looped Hem* Begin by making a buttonhole stitch into the hem. Pass the needle over and under 4 threads, then over the embroidery thread and under the 4 threads of the fabric again. Buttonhole into the opposite edge and repeat from the beginning to the end of the row.

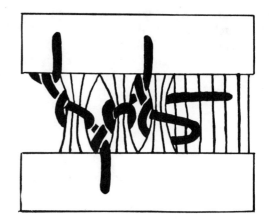

241 *Whipped Hem* Whip a group of threads once (or twice if the border is rather deep). Whip to the opposite side on the next group of threads, and repeat to the end of the row.

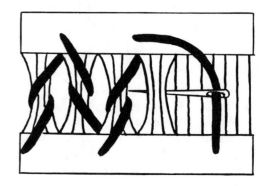

242 *Chained Hem* Work a twisted chain stitch above the border. Move back and work a twisted chain in the centre of a group of threads. Make another twisted chain below the border and on the same threads as the second stitch. Move back and work in the centre of the next group of threads. Repeat from the beginning.

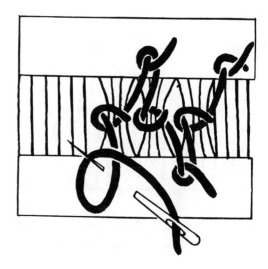

243 *Arrow Head Hem* Begin at A, move 2 threads back and pick up 4. Insert the needle at A and pick up 4 more threads, this time working through the top of the border. Repeat. Work the lower edge in the same way.

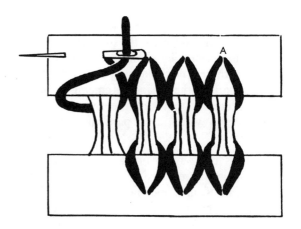

244 *Undulating Hem* Work as for simple hem stitch, but increase the size of the groups of threads and the length of the stitches until the maximum size is reached. Then either drop suddenly to the original size, or decrease gradually to the original size. Repeat.

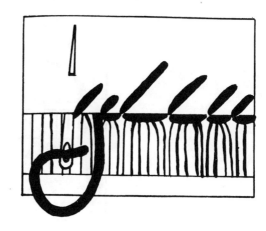

245 *Alternating Twist* was found in a Victorian needlework book, and is an embellishment for the centre of a drawn border. Follow the diagram carefully and repeat 1 and 2 alternately.

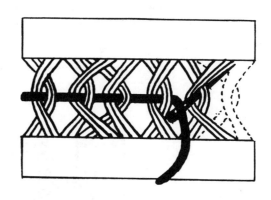

Frayed fringes can be worked on any material, provided that the threads of the fabric slip easily. It is not necessary to confine the shapes to rectangular ones, as it is possible to fray a fringe on round and oval shapes.

Most of the stitches which follow were devised on linen scrim and were fitted into rectangles so that corners could be shown in the diagrams. However, there is no reason why they should not be adapted for other shapes. Remember that it is not necessary to count the threads of the fabric, or to work on a particular group of threads, but the work should be planned and the stitches should be even in size. Planned irregularities are always acceptable.

The diagrams give no idea of the appearance of the finished stitches, as most of them have been drawn on a large scale for the sake of clarity.

246 shows the way to prepare fabric when a frayed fringe is required. First decide on the depth of the fringe, and then withdraw several threads as shown in the diagram. After the stitchery has been worked, the rest of the threads are withdrawn and the fringe is complete.

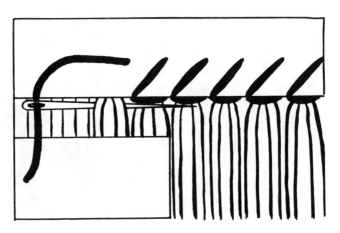

247 *Three-sided Border* shows one row of three-sided stitch worked instead of the hem stitch which is generally used to hold the clusters in place.

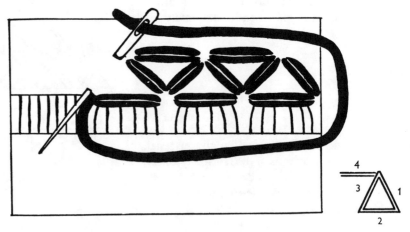

248 *Single Dot* is very easy to work. It is composed of 3 satin stitches which are worked into the same space between the threads of the fabric. Leave several threads between dots. The length of the stitches and the number of threads between groups depends on the weight of the fabric. A corner is shown in the diagram.

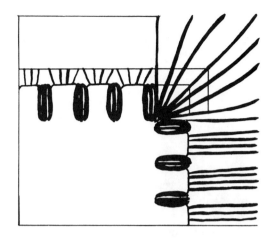

249 *Double Dot* is composed of 2 rows of single dot stitch. Note that the dots are placed one above the other. A corner is shown in the diagram.

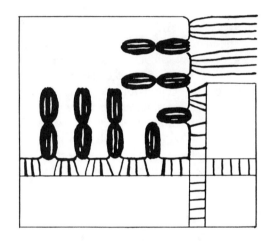

250 *Feathered Edge* is closed feather worked over even numbers of threads. To obtain a neat corner work 3 buttonhole stitches as shown in the diagram, then continue to work closed feather along the next edge.

251 *Closed Herringbone Edge* is easy to work, and at corners simply embroider the top of the stitch only, as is shown in the diagram.

Sometimes neither a hem nor a fringe is required, and there are times when needlepoint edges are not in keeping with the work. Below are two edges which are very strong and firm, and exceedingly attractive when they are worked on even weave, or linen scrim, or any very loosely woven fabric.

252 *Buttonholed Three-sided Edge* Turn a single fold of the material true to a thread and as deep as the first row of stitches. Press, and tack. On the right side work 1 row of three-sided stitch 1 thread below the top of the fold. Work a second row of three-sided stitch below the first one, leaving 1 thread of the fabric between the rows. A row of loops of the fabric will be left on the edge of the fold. Buttonhole into the loops, working enough stitches in each loop to form tiny scallops.

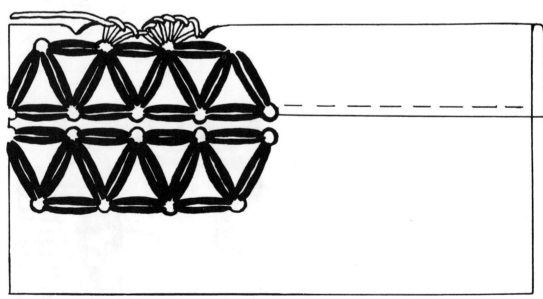

253a and b *Up and Down Edge* Turn a single fold the depth of the first row of stitching and prepare the ground in the same way as for 252. Work a row of up and down buttonhole, leaving the loops between the stitches exactly on the edge of the fold. Work a second row of buttonhole beneath the first. A corner is shown (b). The length of the loop between the corner stitches is not as long as it appears to be. The loops on the edge of the fold may be buttonholed or left unadorned.

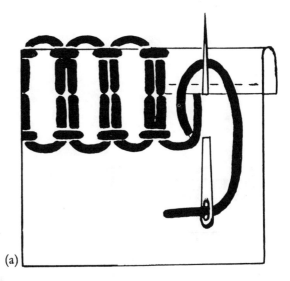

(a)

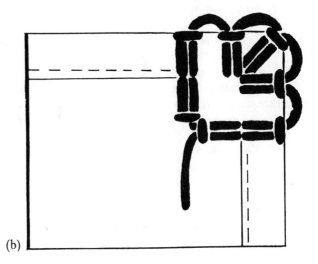

(b)

Canvas Work

Too often the experimentally minded needle-woman thinks of canvas work as a rather dreary occupation. She imagines it consists of a monotonous repetition of stitches worked with woollen threads and that even the choice of stitches is limited to those which are considered to be both durable and suitable. She feels, too, that there is no room for a free interpretation of her design and that every stitch must conform to the weave of the canvas. This is an entirely false impression. Canvas presents a real challenge to the imagination and the only limitation it imposes upon the worker is that of suitability for purpose.

It must be remembered that all fabrics of single and double tabby weave may be used like canvas, and that there are decorative canvases as well as the canvas proper. It is possible to make a canvas-like ground by withdrawing threads from the warp and weft of almost any fabric, be it woollen, silk, cotton or man-made fibres such as nylon and Terylene.

From the very fine to the really coarse ones like thrums and rug canvas, it is possible to obtain results which are pleasing and far from orthodox. The simplest and plainest pieces of work, on any kind of canvas, look alive if different weights of threads are used. Those which are too fine to be used singly can be made into cords, or several strands may be used in the needle instead of one. Coarse threads are usually strong enough to be split and very coarse ones can be couched in various ways with a finer thread.

Different types of thread, metal, raffia, wool, glass, cotton and silk enhance each other and should not be kept rigidly apart. Two different threads of the same colour make even a simple stitch like Smyrna cross look very important. Braids, cords, fringes and tassels, when used with discretion, add an unusual air to canvas work. Tassels, flat and simple, should be knotted round the threads of the background, and hand-made fringes can be added in the same way, so that they become part of the whole scheme.

Sometimes when a piece of work looks dull and flat the addition of a few extra stitches on top of those already there gives the necessary interest. The top stitches need not, indeed should not, be the same as those below. A coarse stitch in a matching colour, even of the same kind of thread as the stitches below, gives a lovely effect. With care a different colour may be used, but a successful result does depend largely on the design. If, for instance, a simple shape has been worked with two rather startling colours, the colour of the top stitchery can act as a binder and subdue a garish effect.

Another interesting method is to work the pattern with flat stitches, and the background with raised ones. It is equally effective to reverse this arrangement, using the raised stitches for the pattern and the flat ones for the background.

The embroiderer might decide to use none of the above-mentioned methods, but to work in a more abstract manner and make greater use of the stitches. One large rice stitch worked in a coarse thread looks most impressive when surrounded with smaller ones worked with a fine thread. Alternatively, a few stitches of a group may be worked with a dull thread to contrast with the rest worked with a bright thread. It is pleasant to vary the effect of dull and bright threads when working composite stitches such as Smyrna cross and Rice stitch. The base of both these stitches is a large cross, and instead of working the whole of a group of large crosses in one kind of thread, use two at least, such as silk and wool. The top stitchery should be reversed, wool on silk and silk on wool.

It is even more fascinating, but perhaps more difficult, to use only one colour. This method calls for a careful choice of the kind and size of stitches and for interesting mixtures of types and weights of threads. The effect of a well-considered piece of one colour is rich yet restrained and it possesses a dignity which is not always to be found in more colourful embroidery.

It is not necessary to cover every thread of the canvas with stitchery and if tiny specks do show between the stitches they add to the tone and texture of the work. In some cases, even when a coarse canvas is being used, a piece of unworked fabric adds to, rather than detracts from, the effect of the whole.

Darning, for instance, looks correct on any kind of canvas, and if a sufficiently soft and thick thread is used, very little of the background will

show. Darning does bind both sides of the canvas firmly, whereas some of the usual stitches do not.

All kinds of beads enrich canvas work, as our Victorian ancestors knew. From the many examples of their work, which are displayed in museums for our delight, we can find much to challenge and inspire us.

Appliqué, with fabrics as different as leather and chiffon, is possible on all sorts of canvas. The pieces may be applied directly to the ground, or upon finished work. Strips of leather may be held in place with open band stitches such as herringbone, and if the ends are not to be oversewn to the fabric, they may be cut into long points and threaded neatly to the back of the work.

Transparent fabrics and nets applied directly to coarse canvas are wonderfully effective. They contrast with heavily worked areas and make delicate grounds for fine stitchery which might not be possible on the canvas alone.

Machine embroidery, especially the linear kind, can be added to canvas work. It is highly decorative, and also acts as a strengthener. For complete success work carefully, and use a coarse machine needle, as the stiff threads of the canvas tend to deflect the needle. This method is suitable for upholstery.

Remember that the barrier which has been erected between canvas work and other forms of embroidery is not real, and many stitches which are considered unsuitable for this kind of work can, and should, be used. Even unlikely ones, such as french knots, look good when worked across the threads of canvas in the manner of Victorian bead work, or when placed upon a plainly stitched ground. Underside couching, as worked in England in the thirteenth century, is ideal for upholstery, as a strong linen couching thread is used. This thread suffers no wear as it is completely hidden at the back of the work. All one has to do is to choose a very durable top thread and to place the couching stitches fairly close together. Rug wool is very hard wearing and is suitable for coarse canvases. If durability is not the first requirement, knobbed, looped or hairy yarns are fun to use and give very pleasant textures.

Looped and pendant couching, composite stitches, feather stitches, chains and back stitches are quite suitable for canvas work, and there are numerous variations of the well-known canvas stitches. I have found that tent stitches and little cross stitches successfully fill any odd spaces and I never encourage people to work fractions of the larger stitches. This method gives a neat finish and an attractive texture to shapes which might otherwise be quite ugly.

The adventurous embroideress will look around for unusual additions to her store of threads, and she will not despise even the humblest offering. Narrow lengths of fabric of different textures and colour (which need not have straight or parallel edges) give the effect of a bold painting when they are threaded in different directions through coarse canvas. Used alone, or in conjunction with other methods, this 'painting' on canvas is well worth while. Gold plate, brass shim, cords and strips of metallic paper may be used either in addition to the strips of fabric or alone.

Plate also looks effective when it is placed on edge in a spiral fashion, rather like a watch spring, either directly on the canvas or on a worked ground.

Flat, round and handle canes have their uses, too. They can be held in place with all kinds of stitches and since they are strong enough to hold a shape without much support, it is not necessary to fix them every inch of the way. Spirals and loops should be left as free as possible.

Orange and cocktail sticks make useful paddings, and need not be covered completely.

Strip cellophane, string of all kinds, knitting and weaving yarns, brass, florists' and even galvanized wire are all useful and have a place in experimental work. Plastic and metal curtain rings, washers, solder, wood veneer, metal rods, pebbles and glass have possibilities which cannot be ignored.

The oddest things look beautiful when used in the right setting, by people who understand their worth. This is clearly shown in the many lovely examples of the embroiderer's ingenuity which are to be found in abundance in our museums today.

Straw, talc and string were used in England in the seventeenth and eighteenth centuries. The Indians used mirror glass in colourful embroidery for shi-sha work, and beetles' wing cases. The Red Indians used birch bark, moose hair and dyed porcupine quills. Even sinews, strips of tin and human hair have found a favoured place in the art of embroidery.

Sometimes the needlewoman, in her enthusiasm, excuses poor workmanship by saying that she has endeavoured to find a new approach. She should try to remember that badly executed embroidery brings all experimental work into disrepute and that many people who would otherwise enjoy using new materials and techniques tend to shun this great adventure because they do not wish to sacrifice their excellent craftsmanship.

Gold Work

Embroidery with metal threads is always regarded with some awe and many people feel it is too difficult for them to attempt. The threads are expensive and the fear of spoiling them and wasting money is often a powerful deterrent. These problems vanish as soon as the embroiderer realizes that many metal threads are easier to handle than lightly twisted silk ones and that the so called 'ruined' thread is invaluable for creating new effects, and should never be discarded as useless. Certainly some metal threads are difficult to manipulate, but so, too, are many other threads which are never regarded with the same amount of apprehension.

I think the most encouraging thing to do is to break all the accepted rules of gold work, and create a piece of embroidery which sparkles with orginality even though it will not bear close inspection.

One great trial for the beginner is the securing of the ends of Japanese gold and passing, and similar threads. She not only wastes a great deal of the precious stuff on the back of the work, but she produces an amateurish effect on the front, with many unwanted bulges and a certain amount of stiffness, to say nothing of inches of

untwisted threads from which loops of the core protrude. She should take a leaf from the book of the Chinese embroiderers, who never dreamed of pulling metal threads through their beautiful silk grounds, but who always, with the greatest skill, began on the right side of the work. It has been my privilege to inspect closely many pieces of Chinese embroidery which are in private collections. I have unpicked the linings of sleevebands, robes and panels, and have never yet discovered any metal thread on the back, but it has always been most difficult to discover the ends of the gold on the front. Since the majority of the pieces are at least 150 years old, one must admit that the method is durable.

Some people dislike metal threads which tarnish, but I think it should be realized that the tarnishing might become a part of the future beauty of the work. It is said that 'the Chinese used to embroider today with their eyes on tomorrow', knowing full well that the brilliant colours they were using would fade in time to the wonderful tones which we admire so much today.

We know that in the past, English embroiderers would polish gold work with dried bread crumbs, and that varnishing was, and is still, used to good effect. We can buy gold which tarnishes very slowly or not at all, but I do feel that tarnished gold should not always be despised.

Japanese Gold is guaranteed not to tarnish. It is spun on a silk core, and can be obtained in many different thicknesses, or as cords which are pliable and not as bright as the plain thread. For centuries this thread has been used for simple outlining, for solid and semi-solid fillings, and for handsome but rather stiff raised work. In the East, in Europe and in England it was often couched with coloured silks. This method gave rise to shot and shaded effects, which effectively subdued the brilliance of the gold. It is especially interesting when the spaces between the couching stitches vary considerably, and good use of this idea has resulted in some exciting modern pieces.

In these days when very lovely backgrounds are so easy to obtain, it is a pity to place the rows of gold very close together. Rather open them out to expose the beauty beneath, or to make room for beads or stitchery.

In every case either coloured or yellow couching threads may be used. It must be mentioned in passing that it is not always necessary to couch double threads of Japanese gold. Again we must examine old Chinese works, where, it will be noted, single strands of gold were often used to the exclusion of double ones. These single strands were used to outline fine silk and canvas work and as solid and semi-solid fillings on robes. It is often easier to handle a single strand, and I have no hesitation in recommending this method.

254–7 *Gold Basket Work* The basket pattern worked with Japanese gold is much admired, but it does tend to make a rather formal filling. Where the formality can be dispensed with, use gold cord, silk cord, and imitation gold in place of the usual string padding, and open out the rows of top stitching in order to show this interesting arrangement
Interesting result can be achieved by varying the size of the cords used for padding from very fine to quite coarse, instead of using cords of equal thickness.

Another method is to fill only part of any given shape with basket pattern and to leave the rest of the filling flat.

254 *Closed basket pattern*

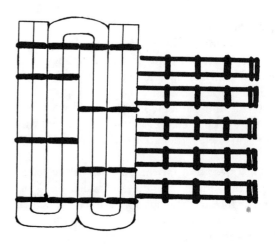

255 *Open basket on silk cord*

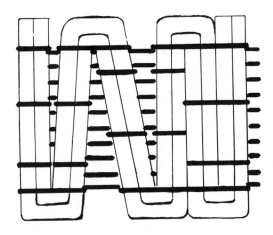

256 *Uneven padding*

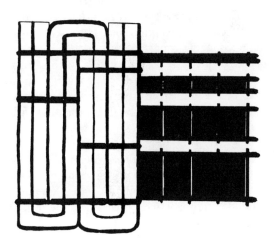

257 *Partly padded shape*

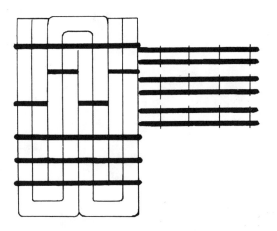

Gold Purls are spun like hollow tubes and are very pliable and easily pulled open. These threads are usually cut into smallish pieces and the pieces are threaded upon fine silk and sewn down like beads. They can be curled into horse-shoe shapes and used also for couching metal and silk cords and for attaching sequins. Very small left-overs can be used for seeding. I have found it possible to work the basket pattern, and serpentine and pendant couching with purls. The method is rewarding but it does need care. Because these threads are hollow the couching stitches should not be pulled tight unless a broken effect in the line of gold is desired.

The last sentence brings us to the deliberate destruction of these threads in order to create a new effect. Pull a length of purl fairly wide open before couching it in some way, either plain, or looped, or pendant or serpentine. Couch it from side to side across a border, leaving it free to sway, or pull it apart in a prearranged pattern to make it look like a row of bugles alternating with spirals.

Pearl Purls are hollow tubes which are spun in such a way that they resemble a string of round gold beads. These threads are often used for outlining and for lettering. It is possible to pull

them open and re-wind on knitting needles, if a loose but heavy curled effect is required. Pull them apart in the ways which have been suggested for purl, and use them over paddings and for seeding. Pearl purls are more difficult to manage than purls, but with care and patience several methods of couching are possible. The couching stitch becomes invisible if, when one is using pearl purl in its natural state, one pulls the little beads gently open to allow the thread to disappear inside the tube.

Plate is a flat strip of gold which can be couched flat, or kinked by pressing it into the grooves of a butter pat (or a screw, or hair comb) and it can even be used for the basket pattern. It looks most effective when it is zigzagged over a padding of orange sticks or string (258a and b), but care must be taken when folding the strip, because it snaps easily. If the thread or the needle is placed over the plate before folding it, the strain on the gold will be eased. A tighter fold can be obtained by pressing gently on the plate with the thimble. Wind it carefully round a knitting needle for a curled effect.

Plate looks enchanting when it is couched with purl (259), especially if the couching is done in an irregular manner. Broken pieces may be pierced with a strong needle and sewn down with a bead.

258 Plate zigzagged over padding

a—string

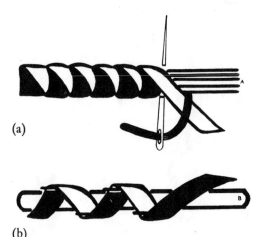

(a)

b—orange stick or coloured cord   (b)

259 Plate couched with purl

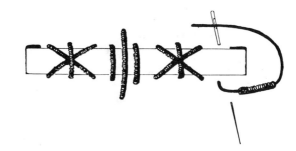

Plate looks interesting if it is looped upwards between the couching stitches, or if it is lifted by placing bugles under it at regular intervals and couched between them. The ends may be cut to points or given other shapes, but before beginning a long row of couching it may be necessary to make a tiny hook by turning the end under and placing a holding stitch in the fold.

Try spiral plate, set on its edge like a watch spring. This looks good on wall hangings and is effective on all kinds of fabric, including canvas.

Passing is spun tightly round a silk core and is obtainable in several thicknesses, the finest being known as tambour. It is possible to stitch with most passing threads provided the needle has a large enough eye to protect the metal from fraying. A certain amount of springiness must be expected, and accepted as a characteristic of the thread. One finds stitchery with a thread like passing on *Opus Anglicanum* and on Chinese work. This strong thread will hold a shape quite well, and it deserves more freedom than it is usually given. Loops need only be held with one couching stitch, provided the stitch is firm and is made with a strong thread. Any portions of the thread which become untwisted and separated from the core should be saved and used like open purl.

Do allow gold thread a reasonable amount of freedom, as it falls into such lovely lines when it is not strained. Instead of outlining a shape with an even number of rows set tightly together, try the effect of working say two and a half times round, and allow the lines to separate in places.

Partial outlines give sparkle in important places and a slipped one adds distinction to an otherwise dull shape.

Make use of staggered couching to vary the thickness of an outline, or use a looped line alternately with a straight one. Plate and purl, or pearl purl and passing used alternately on outlines give richness and interest which is lacking in flat, straight ones.

For a light filling work round and round a shape, from the outside, inwards. Vary the distance between the lines, and allow them to meet in one or two places. Couch with one colour, a matching colour, or several colours. Added interest is given if the thickness of the couching thread is gradually increased as the work progresses.

Although extended couching requires no enrichment (see page 79), the embroiderer who has acquired skill and who feels really confident of her ablity to use colour might like to add to her work. Small pieces of fabric, applied to the ground before the couching is begun, look very pleasing. It is possible to couch the gold with coloured thread but this is one case in which the addition of colour seems, to me, to detract from the beauty of the work. Purls, passing, pearl purl and cords work very well but I feel that Japanese gold, except the very finest, is not really suitable.

Break up the monotony of large expanses of gold by adding small pieces of padding in unexpected places and change the direction of the thread often.

Most gold threads, even the slippery purls, can be plaited, knitted, corded and crocheted. A large hook is best for crochet. The thickness of these hand-made cords can be varied by beginning with several threads and gradually reducing the number until only one is left. Remember that all these plaits and cords should be couched in such a way that they are never strained. Do not reserve them for edges only.

If hand methods do not give the required effect, a zigzag sewing machine might do so. The width of the zigzag and the length of the stitch can be altered as desired. A loose needle tension, a large needle and a long stitch make it possible to top sew with fine gold passing, and this method looks exactly like underside couching.

Expensive gold threads are not always required, and some of these ideas are equally suitable for Japanese silver, aluminium and imitation gold and silver threads. All these threads may be mixed with the expensive ones or used alone. It is possible to stitch with some of these threads; even the narrow flat Lurex which is sold on reels works well on fairly loosely woven fabrics. Some of these threads can be hand-wound on a sewing machine bobbin. If a loose shuttle tension is used with a very tight needle tension, the metal appears on the right side of the work in a series of tiny loops which resemble a loose cord. The result is best when the feed dog is lowered and foot either removed or replaced with a darning foot. For those who prefer to machine in the usual manner, it is better to keep the tensions normal (although it might be necessary to loosen the shuttle), and to place the work with the wrong side uppermost. The metal will show on the right side.

Finally, do not be afraid to pile one kind of gold over another instead of using any other form of padding. With care it is possible to sew over all kinds of gold stitchery and the effect is very rich indeed.

It is not necessary to use expensive silk and velvet backgrounds for metal threads. There are so many glass, raffia, cotton, woollen and canvas fabrics which are a perfect foil for the high gloss of gold threads, and I feel that their possibilities have not yet been fully explored. A backing of Dowlais or some similar material is necessary in most cases because it helps to support the weight of the threads and prevents puckering.

Since there are so many good books on both gold and canvas work I have not attempted to teach methods, but I have tried to stimulate the imagination, to remove barriers and to persuade ambitious needlewomen that good technique and a creative approach to embroidery are not opponents but inseparable companions.

As we gaze in awe and admiration upon embroideries, created long years ago, which have found their way into public and private collections, it is humbling to think that some of our work might be subject to the same close scrutiny and speculation by people to whom this twentieth century will seem dim and unreal.

We owe much to our ancestors, the professionals, the amateurs and the children, who laboured with the needle, and whose thoughts were doubtless centred upon immediate events, and who never probed into the distant future.

We owe a great deal to posterity also, and whilst we are happily creating new works with our needles, I think we should try to achieve embroidery upon which our descendants will look with pride, and historians will be pleased to expend both their time and their talents.

Index